Go for IT!

PETER BISHOP

Hodder & Stoughton

LONDON SYDNEY AUCKLAND TORONTO

Publisher's acknowledgements

The publishers would like to thank the following for their permission to reproduce copyright photographs:

Abatron 54 (right); Action-Plus Photographic 13 (top); Barclays Bank 43 (middle), 84 (bottom right); Barnaby's Picture Library 13 (middle right), 15 (middle right, bottom right), 40 (middle left), 94 (top left, top right), 100 (bottom), 124 (right); Birmingham International Airport 121 (top left); British Rail 55 (middle); Canon (UK) Ltd 19 (right); Epson (UK) Ltd 19 (left); Ford Motor company 121 (bottom left); GeoScience Features Picture Library 22 (left); Greenpeace/Lejeunes 15 (top); Griffin and George 93 (top), 114 (bottom); HMSO 33; Hotpoint Ltd 121 (top right); International Stock Exchange Photo Library 1 (top, middle right, bottom right), 2 (top), 4 (middle), 13 (bottom), 15 (middle left), 18 (bottom), 20, 32 (bottom left), 40 (middle right, bottom left, bottom right), 54 (left), 57 (middle right), 64 (bottom), 70, 72 (top), 80 (left, right), 81, 84 (top left, top right, bottom left), 89 (bottom left, bottom right), 91 (top), 99, 100 (top, middle), 111, 112 (all), 113 (top), 114 (top), 121 (bottom right), 125 (top), 126 (top); London Fire Brigade 13 (middle left); Manchester University 123; Metropolitan Police 15 (bottom left), 88; Micrograf International 54 (middle); MSW Rapp Collins 1 (bottom left); National Westminster Bank plc 126 (bottom); NEC 42 (bottom right); Oxfam/M. McClean 22 (right); Picture Point — London 97; Post Office 67; Research Machines cover, 2 (middle bottom), 3 (top), 4 (top, bottom left, bottom right), 5, 47 (all), 51, 56 (all), 57 (top, middle left), 95, 96 (top left, top right, middle), 107, 108, 127 (top left, top middle, top right); Roland Digital Group 64 (top); Rover Group 125 (bottom); Safeways plc 60 (top); Science Photo Library 8, 32 (bottom right), 42 (bottom left); Sonia Halliday Photographs 101 (top); TeleFocus — British Telecom Photographs 1 (middle left), 72 (bottom), 75, 76; Tesco plc 129 (top); Thomas Cook Group 129 (bottom); Vivien Fifield Picture Library 124 (left).

The publishers would also like to thank the following for their help in the production of this book:

Ian Lishman (International Stock Exchange Photo Library); Alleyn's School, Dulwich; *Just Seventeen; Smash Hits; Green Magazine; Marie Clare.*

British Library Cataloguing in Publication Data
Bishop, Peter 1949–
    Go for it!
    1. Information systems
    I. Title
    001.5

ISBN 0-340-52656-4

First Published 1990

Typeset by Peter Bishop Associates.

Printed in Great Britain for the educational publishing division of Hodder and Stoughton Ltd, Mill Road, Dunton Green, Sevenoaks, Kent by Cambus Litho, East Kilbride.

Contents

Preface

Information Technology (IT), the product of a worldwide technological revolution, is now caught up in another revolution within UK education — the implementation of the National Curriculum. The main effect of this is the dispersal of IT throughout secondary schools, to become a service facility wherever it can effectively be used. Its aim is set out clearly in the National Curriculum document on Technology (March 1990):

> 'Pupils should be able to use information technology to:
>
> ▶ communicate and handle information
>
> ▶ design, develop, explore and evaluate models of real or imaginary situations
>
> ▶ measure physical quantities and control movement.
>
> They should be able to make informed judgements about the application and importance of information technology, and its effect on the quality of life.'   (IT Capability Attainment Target)

Go For IT! is a response to this requirement. It is an IT activities book, intended for use in a variety of subject areas, for a variety of purposes, working with a variety of information and software to handle this information. Its mission is to enable pupils to experience the benefits of IT at first hand, performing a range of interesting and challenging tasks, many of which would be impracticable without IT. In the process, a number of vital skills are taught: at one level, the ability to use IT systems confidently; and at another level, the ablity to plan tasks and implement these plans, both individually and in groups, making the best use of available resources.

Go For IT! is intended for pupils of all abilities in the 14-16 age range (Key State 4 in National Curriculum terminology). Until the National Curriculum is fully operational at Key Stage 4, many pupils will need simple and straightforward activities. Accordingly, **Go For IT!** provides these as well as more advanced activities. The flexible nature of the book makes it easily adaptable to a level suited to the abilities and interests of the pupils, the level of experience and training of the teacher, and the computing equipment available.

In addition to responding to the needs of the National Curriculum, **Go For IT!** remains true to its roots — the rapid, continuing spread of IT throughout the workplace, and the consequent need for a generation of computer-literate school leavers and graduates. IT awareness and capability are vital skills in the late twentieth century, opening many doors to both professional and personal achievement.

Objectives

In response to these requirements, **Go For IT!** has the following objectives:

1 To provide a practical introduction to the use of information technology in a variety of situations.

2 To cover a range of activities which are:

> ► **realistic** in relation to the use of IT in commerce and industry

> ► **relevant** to the knowledge, ability and interests of typical 14 to 16 year-old pupils

> ► **useful** for a wide range of tasks which would otherwise have to be done manually at school (or could not realistically be attempted without IT)

> ► **cross-curricular** covering a range of school topic areas, concentrating on core topics in the National Curriculum

> ► **challenging** in that they extend and enhance pupils' skills and experience.

3 To give pupils practice in solving practical problems with the assistance of IT.

4 To give pupils confidence in the operation of common IT tools, in particular: word processors, spreadsheets, databases, graphics packages, viewdata systems, electronic mail, control systems and desktop publishing packages.

5 To provide practical evidence of the significant benefits — savings of cost, time, resources, etc. — which are gained by the use of IT in a wide range of applications. Also to demonstrate how new activities become possible which could not be done before the introduction of IT.

6 To provide an insight into the nature of information, how to organise information, and gain access to it, and demonstrate the capabilities, limitations and wider implications of IT in dealing with information.

Structure

The general structure of the text is based on a series of **activities**, approximately three per IT topic area, graduated as follows:

Introductory: short, specific, guided activities, with sample computer screens and typical inputs shown at each stage, and a prescribed outcome shown in the text. Suitable for small groups or individual pupil work.

Intemediate: more substantial activities described in less detail, with the general outcome specified. The full design of the implementation of the IT system is given in the text. Suitable for small group work.

Advanced: larger, more open-ended activities, suitable either for a group, or as a project, either in IT or another subject, if undertaken by an individual pupil. The activities require outside research and information gathering, and detailed design by the pupil(s). The steps are described in general terms only, and a range of possible outcomes is suggested.

The activities are complemented by exercises giving further suggestions for IT activities, in outline only. Exercises fall into all of the above categories. The exercise in the chapter on combined IT topics includes a set of project suggestions.

Each IT topic area is associated with a brief section on the feature of the IT system most relevant to the topic. IT features include input, output, and storage devices, communications networks, microcomputers and special-purpose microchips in common use. These are covered in outline only, from the point of view of a user, with the emphasis on their suitability for particular types of tasks, and the benefits they provide. No technical details are included.

Also associated with certain of the IT activities are a small number of short sections on the general nature of information; covering aspects of collecting, arranging, managing and accessing information, and issues such as the accuracy, reliability and confidentiality of information.

In conclusion is a general chapter, Why IT?. This draws some general conclusions from the previous material about the suitability of IT for a range of activities, and the benefits to be gained from its use.

The small number of technical IT terms used are described in the Glossary at the back of the book.

IT Equipment

It is recognised that there is an ever-changing range of hardware, software and electronic equipment in use in UK secondary schools. **Go For IT!** is independent of any particular computers, software and electronic equipment. The activities are designed to be implemented on the types of IT equipment commonly available. Instructions are given in general terms, and points where some difficulties may be encountered are highlighted by a specific request to consult the user guide for the particular software item in use.

It is realised that the interpretation of these general instructions in terms of specific operations on a particular piece of software is something of a challenge for the teacher. To overcome this, a certain amount of preparatory work is recommended, possibly including the drafting of short supplementary worksheets to get the pupils going on their own systems. Experience indicates that, once the initial confidence is gained in the use of the system, pupils progress rapidly.

Teacher's Book

A change in curriculum of this magnitude in a short space of time places a great strain on the teachers. **Go For IT!** is intended to be used by teachers from many subject disciplines, most of whom are assumed to be newcomers to IT. A certain amount of assistance in classroom planning and class management is included in the text, and all activities have been carefully planned to include work done away from the computer. One microcomputer per four or five pupils in a class should cope with most activities.

In addition, to give the teacher some advice on the use of the book, a separate **Teacher's Book** is provided. This gives suggested subject areas for the activities, hints on class organisation and the management of computing and other resources, answers to all exercise questions which have a specific answer, and a list of software which can be used for the activities in the book.

Acknowledgements

A number of people have been of great assistance in the planning, development and checking of this book. I am particularly grateful to my reviewers, Tim Denning, Steve Bacon, Dave Futcher and Joe Telford for their advice and comments at the planning stage, and during the drafting of material. I am also grateful to Chris Jennings of Research Machines for ideas and assistance in the drawing and design chapters, and in the preparation of screen photographs used as illustrations. My thanks also go to Sarah Bishop and Jenny Davies for checking drafts and administrative assistance.

The text was prepared on an RM Nimbus PC-186 computer, using the WordStar word processor and PC Paintbrush and Micrografx Designer drawing programs. Text was typeset using Aldus Pagemaker directly from the word processor output, and transferred to a Linotronic printer for final masters. In view of the complexity of the design, page makeup was done manually.

Peter Bishop

1990

CHAPTER 1

Introduction

Go for IT! is all about **computers**, **communications** and **control systems**, together known as **information technology** or **IT** for short. It introduces you to a number of practical ways to use (and benefit from) the new technology, without going into any technical details.

Before you start, it is important to remind you of a few important things about computers: what they consist of, what they do, and how they can be linked together. Now is also a good time to remind you of a few special words used in connection with information technology. If when reading this book, you cannot remember what one of these words means, you will find it in this chapter, or in the Glossary at the back of the book.

This chapter also poses a question — 'Why has IT become so important?' The answer is not found in this chapter; you will answer it as you work through the book. The last chapter discusses it fully.

▶ Information technology in action. IT is now used to help us in many of the things we do.

SECTION 1A

What is a Computer?

A computer can be described as an **information processing machine**.

▶ **Information** is what we see, hear, speak, draw or write down. It can be in the form of letters, numbers, drawings, sounds, or any combination of these. Information is the raw material of computers.

▶ **Processing** is what a computer does with information. It includes sorting, selecting, combining and re-arranging information, and doing calculations. Computers can also make simple decisions based on information.

▶ Using the word **machine** means that computers can be grouped with car engines, washing machines, sewing machines, etc. Machines are devices which do useful work. Like all machines computers need to be controlled carefully, and can break down.

You can also describe a computer as a **digital, electronic** device which can be **programmed**.

▶ **Digital** means that a computer works with numbers, letters, sounds and pictures represented as digits. Pictures are stored as grids of dots, like a television picture. The colour of each dot is coded as a number. Sounds are stored as sequences of numbers.

▶ **Electronic** describes the way that computers are made from **microchips** (also called **integrated circuits** or **ICs**). Microchips contain very small electric circuits where information is stored and processed. They are made from silicon, which is found in sand. They work very fast, and have no moving parts.

▶ A **program** is a set of instructions which make the computer do a task. For example, if you want to use a computer for word processing, you first load a word processing program. Once a program has been loaded into a computer, it carries out the instructions automatically, at great speed. In this book, you do **not** have to know how programs are produced, nor how they work. The aim is to teach you how to use them.

Programs are also known as **software**, to distinguish them from the electronic devices which make up a computer, which are called **hardware**.

▶ The commonest type of computer — a personal computer (PC) — is used on the desk in most offices, and in many schools, colleges and universities.

▶ A computer screen can show text and pictures. The pictures are stored as patterns of dots.

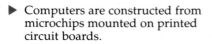

▶ Computers are constructed from microchips mounted on printed circuit boards.

SECTION 1B — *What Can a Computer Do?*

A computer can do seven types of tasks, all to do with information. They are **input**, **output**, **storing**, **retrieving**, **sending**, **receiving** and **processing**. In the activities in this book, you will make a computer do all these types of tasks.

▶ **Input** is getting information into a computer. The commonest way of doing this is to type the information at a keyboard.

▶ **Output** is getting information out of a computer. This can be done by displaying it on the screen or printing it.

▶ **Storing** is making a permanent copy of the information that the computer can use again later. The commonest way of storing information is on a magnetic disk.

▶ **Retrieving** is getting information back from the place where it has been stored.

▶ **Sending** is transferring information to another computer. The computers may be linked on a **network** in the same building, or they may be many miles apart, linked by telephone lines or satellite links. Section 1D has more details about networks.

▶ **Receiving** is picking up information from another computer.

▶ **Processing** is what a computer does with the information, as described in the previous section.

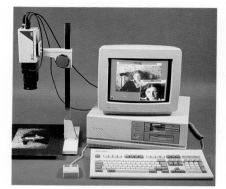

▶ This computer is taking in the image from a video camera as input, and displaying the same image as output.

SECTION 1C — *The Parts of a Computer*

Computers are made in all shapes and sizes, but the ones you use look like the one shown in the photograph. They are given the name **microcomputers** (sometimes shortened to **micros**) because they are based on a processor made from a single microchip.

▶ The parts of a typical microcomputer. Larger computers are made up of separate units, often in several rooms, but they have the same parts.

processor — memory — Winchester disk — keyboard

display screen — printer — magnetic disk drive — mouse

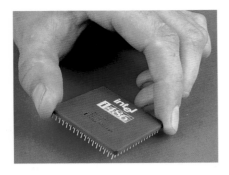

▶ Processing and memory chips.

The parts of a computer which you use are as follows:

▶ The **keyboard** is for typing information (input). It is similar to a typewriter keyboard.

▶ The **mouse** is a small, hand-held device which you move over the surface of your desk, making a pointer move on the display screen. The mouse is used to control the computer, and for drawing on the screen (input).

▶ The **display screen** is for displaying information (output). It works like a television set, and can display both text and pictures.

▶ The **processor** is the single microchip inside the computer where the information is processed.

▶ The **memory** is a set of microchips which store information and instructions while they are being processed. The memory is not used for permanent storage.

▶ The **magnetic disk drive** is used for storage and retrieval of information. The disks can be removed from the drive, and kept until they are needed again.

▶ The **Winchester disk** is a permanent, high-capacity disk used for storing information and programs.

▶ A magnetic disk and two Winchester disks.

▶ The **printer** is an output device which makes permanent copies of the information from the computer.

▶ The **network cable** is used for sending and receiving data around the network of computers. Computers do not have to be connected to a network, but they are much more useful if they are.

In later sections of this book, the parts of a computer listed in this section are described in more detail.

SECTION 1D | *Networks*

Information technology is all about getting the right information to the right place at the right time. Computers store and process the information, and are linked to **networks** to get the information to the place where it is needed.

There are three types of network in common use. **Local networks**, where all the computers in one building (school, office, factory, hospital, etc.), are connected by cables. **Long-distance networks** connect computers over long distances, usually via telephone lines. The third type of network links **terminals** to central computers. Terminals are input/output devices, without processing facilities. General-purpose terminals have keyboards and screens, special-purpose terminals include cash terminals at supermarkets and banks, and monitoring devices in factories. See Figures 1.1, 1.2 and 1.3.

Local and long-distance networks allow computers to share expensive items such as Winchester disks and laser printers. These are controlled by central computers, called **servers,** which make the shared items available to all the other computers, known as **workstations,** on the network. The use of central servers reduces costs, and makes it easier for users to share programs and exchange information.

▶ A local network of computers in an office. It is similar to the networks found in many schools.

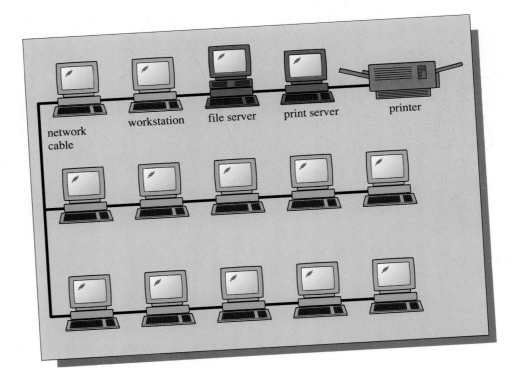

▶ Figure 1.1: A local network, showing how the servers and workstations are connected.

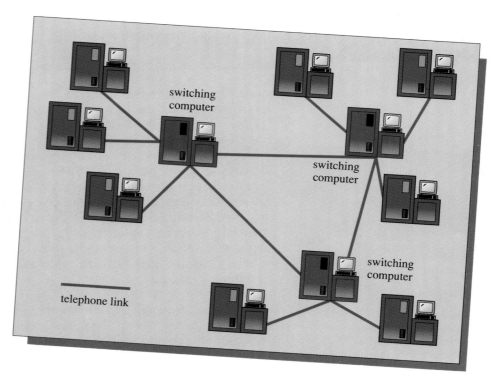

▶ Figure 1.2: A long-distance network using telephone lines. Central computers are used to switch the messages from senders to receivers.

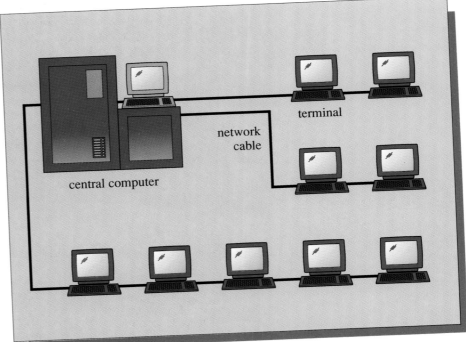

▶ Figure 1.3: A network of terminals connected to a central computer. The terminals are used for input and output only, the computer does all the processing.

The combination of computers and networks enables IT to provide a range of services which are of great benefit to the people who use them. They are essential for the operation of many organisations, as you will find out in later chapters of this book.

SECTION 1E *Control Systems*

Years ago, washing machines had switches to turn them on and off, to fill them up and empty them, and to turn the water heater on and off. These switches had to be operated by hand in the right order whenever a load of washing was being done. This took up a lot of time, and made it difficult to get the washing done well. Modern washing machines are **automatic**. They follow a sequence of instructions without someone having to press a switch at each stage. There is a different program for each type of washing. This means that the washing is done better, with less effort, than with the old type of washing machine.

Automatic control is built into many household devices today. Some examples include microwave ovens, central heating systems, compact disk players and video recorders. In factories, robots and automatic controls on machines are used extensively. Ships, aircraft and some trains have automatic controls. Traffic lights and automatic doors are a few more examples of automatic control.

Most automatic control systems are made up from the same types of microchips as are used in computers and communications systems. Computers, communications and automatic control systems are often used together. For example, an air traffic control system uses communications to locate the aircraft and for the controllers to talk to the pilots; computers to keep a record of the identities of the planes, and to check that their paths are safe; and automatic control systems to guide the planes as they approach airport runways. All these sytems are based on microchips.

Automatic control does not mean that people have no say at all in what happens. For example, a person chooses the program for an automatic washing machine, and air traffic is controlled by people, with the aid of information technology. Automatic control takes care of all the routine steps, leaving people to take the key decisions. It has led to great improvements in efficiency and safety, and many activities and devices — air traffic control and compact disk players to name just two — would not be possible without microchips.

EXERCISE 1

Questions

1 Write down the names of **two** types of each of the following:

   (a) input devices

   (b) output devices

   (c) storage devices.

2 A computer is not the only type of device which can be programmed. Make a list of as many others as you can.

3 Why are small computers called microcomputers?

4 How do two computers, which are thousands of miles apart, communicate with each other?

5 (a) What are the **three** types of computer network?

(b) What are the benefits of computer networks?

6 (a) What is the main aim of information technology?

(b) How do computers and networks help to achieve this aim?

7 (a) Make lists of as many uses of automatic control as you can think of:

in the home

in offices

in factories.

(b) Choose **three** of these, and, for each one:

say what manual device (if any) the automatic system has replaced

list the advantages of automatic control in this application.

8 (a) List some activities which combine all three aspects of IT: computers, communications and control systems.

(b) Choose **one** of these, and list the benefits which arise from the combination of the three aspects.

9 From what you have read in this chapter, give some reasons for the widespread use of information technology.

Things to Find Out

1 Find out the names and brief details of some popular microcomputers. In what ways are they similar, and how do they differ?

2 The keyboard and mouse are not the only types of input devices used by computers. Find out about some other input and output devices which are in use.

3 Find out about some types of output device not mentioned in the text. For each one, find out what it is used for, and the advantages it has over other types of output device for these uses.

4 A type of storage which is coming into use is **optical disks** (also known as **CD-ROMs**). Find out some uses of optical disks, and their advantages and disadvantages over magnetic disks.

▶ An optical disk, also known as a CD-ROM, which can store very large amounts of information.

Things to Do

1 Find some pictures of different types of computers. If possible, obtain a range from small to large computers. Try to identify the parts of each computer.

2 If you were to have a computer at home, decide what types of input and output devices you would like. Make a list of the equipment you would choose, and give brief reasons for the choice of each item. Also try to find out how much each item would cost.

Alternatively, if you already have a home computer, list the items it is made up of, and write down what you use each one for. Then list any additional items you would like, and the uses you would make of them. Find out how much these additional items would cost.

CHAPTER 2

Word Processing

Word processing (often referred to by its initials **WP**) is using a computer to handle text, for example letters, documents, articles, books, etc. Most microcomputers use a program for word processing; a few, known as word processors, are set up to do nothing but word processing. Whichever type is used, WP enables you to:

▶ Type text at the computer keyboard. What you have typed appears on the screen, in the same layout as it will be printed.

▶ Save what you have typed on disk. A piece of text is referred to as a **document**. Each document is identified by a name, which you give it when you first create it.

▶ Retrieve a document from disk. You enter the name of the document to identify it.

▶ Correct and modify existing documents. This is the great advantage of word processors — you do not have to retype documents when you are correcting them.

▶ Print documents. A document may be printed at any stage, whether it is a rough draft or the final version.

Some word processors have facilities to save parts of documents separately, and include these into other documents. They can also merge the text of letters with lists of names and addresses, creating a letter addressed individually to each person on the list. Printing can be single or double spaced: single spacing saves paper, but double spacing makes drafts easier to correct.

Word processing is used in many businesses, where it has replaced the use of typewriters for producing letters, contracts, reports, advertisements and memos. It is also used by authors to write books (this book was produced using a word processing program), and by translators. Over the last few years newspapers have changed to word processors for the reporters to type their stories.

The benefits of word processing are its speed and flexibility. Documents can be corrected and changed as often as is necessary, and printed whenever required. There is no need to make additional copies of a document, as it can be stored on disk to be looked at or printed at a later date. Most people find word processing easy to learn — it takes only a few hours to become confident.

ACTIVITY 2A   *Job Application*

In this activity, you will use word processing to produce a letter applying for a job. You will do it in **three** stages:

Wanted: Young person as office assistant in expanding company. Needs general office skills, word processing, good telephone manner. Good pay, pleasant working conditions in modern office, promotion prospects. Applications to: Mr R. Jones, Personnel Department, Speedbird Distributors, PO Box 4357, Milton Keynes MK3 5TG.

Sales assistants required. Young people's clothes shop has several vacancies. We are looking for lively young people with a pleasant manner, neat and tidy and good with figures. Good pay for the right people. Applications to: Ms Judy Simmonds, DownTown Clothes, High Street, Salford M56 7RQ.

Receptionist wanted for international company. We require an energetic person with a good telephone manner, a sound knowledge of English and some French. A third European language would be an added benefit. Competitive salary and additional responsibilities, company benefits. Apply to: Joanna York, TransEurope Finance, West Point House, Bracknell BR7 9UH.

Trainee technicians required. Electronics company seeks technicians for assembly and testing of our wide range of electronic products. Knowledge of maths and physics essential, must be able to work carefully with only occasional supervision. Day release for further training. Good pay and excellent promotion prospects. Write to: Mr G. J. Westbury, JJ Electronics, Huntsforth Estate, Cambridge CB5 3DX.

Travelling theatre company needs help! We are looking for someone who can make order out of chaos, beg for costumes and props, arrange places to stay, help pack equipment and lights, and mend things when they break down. Must stay cheerful whatever happens. Sounds impossible? Maybe it's just the challenge you've been looking for. Contact Rosemary Butler, Strolling Players, 37 Frith Street London WC3 9JJ.

▶ Some typical job advertisements — which one is for you?

▶ a plan of the letter

▶ a first draft

▶ the final copy which you would send.

You will work on your own for this activity, but be prepared to share the computer with others!

1 Choose **one** of the job advertisements and imagine that you are going to apply for the job it describes.

2 Start up the word processing program on your computer.

3 Open up a document for your letter. Give the document a name, such as the one below, replacing the XX with your own initials:

XXJOBAPP

4 The computer screen shows a blank area where your letter will appear as you type it. Don't worry about making mistakes, they are easy to correct.

At the top left of the screen is a flashing mark, or a bright square. This is called the **cursor**. It shows where the next character you type will appear. After you have typed some text, you can use the arrow keys to move the cursor around the text.

5 Type the plan of your letter, setting out the main points you wish to make. One possible layout is shown in the screen below, but you do not have to follow it exactly.

```
                                        Home Address
                                        Date

Name
Address

Dear ...

Reference to the job

School subjects

Interests and hobbies

Reasons for applying for the job

Yours sincerely
```

▶ Plan of job application letter.

6 If you make a mistake, move the cursor to the right of the wrong character(s), and press the Delete key to remove it. Then type the corrections.

7 When you have checked and corrected the plan, save the document on disk, close it (if this is a separate operation on your word processor) and print it. Give someone else a turn at the computer.

8 Away from computer, check the printed copy of the plan, and decide what you are going to write. Pencil in some key words under the points you have printed.

9 Back at the computer, start up the word processor again (if necessary), and open up the plan of your letter. You will need to type the name you gave the document when you created it.

10 Move the cursor to each point in the plan, delete it, and type the text in its place. Use the letter below as an example, but do **not** copy it.

```
                                    21 Washford Crescent
                                    Ashbury
                                    Gloucestershire    GL8 6YT
                                    25th March 1989
Ms Rosemary Butler
Strolling Players
37 Frith Street
London WC3 9JJ

Dear Ms Butler

I am writing to apply for the job as helper in your theatre
company.

I am a pupil at Ashbury School, studying English, French, Art,
History, Environmental Studies and Maths. I am taking GCSE exams
in these subjects this summer, and I hope to get good grades.

I am very interested in the theatre. I am in the school drama
group, and was Lady Macbeth last Christmas. I have been in a
number of other plays, and helped with lights, costumes and
scenery. We go to the theatre in Gloucester quite often, and
this Easter we went to London to see Cats. I am sorry to say
that I haven't seen your theatre group.

My other hobbies are music and dancing, and I help at an old
people's home on Saturdays.

I am used to coping with chaos - there is plenty of it in our
house. I am always having to fix things that my two younger
sisters have broken. I like meeting people and helping out. I am
sure that I could cope with the job.

Yours sincerely

Emma Gibson
```

▶ Draft of job application letter.

11 When you have typed your first draft, move the cursor to the top of the screen, and then run it down the letter as you check it. Correct any mistakes you find.

12 Save your letter on disk, close the document and print it. Give someone else a turn at the computer.

13 Read the printed copy of the draft carefully, and mark any mistakes, or places where the wording could be improved.

14 Back at the computer, start the word processing program (if necessary) and call up your letter.

15 Make the corrections you marked on the draft, and check the letter on the screen. Make sure that you correct **all** the mistakes, and do not introduce any others.

16 Save and close down the document, and print the final copy of the letter.

This is the way that many business letters are produced: a plan of the points, a first draft and then the final copy. Word processing makes it easy to correct mistakes, and to make changes, without the need for any re-typing.

ACTIVITY 2B *Magazine Article*

In this activity you will write an article for a magazine, using word processing. The article is about a recent event such as a sports match or school play, or an accident such as a fire which has happened locally. There are three stages in the process:

▶ rough notes in your notebook

▶ a first draft

▶ a final draft.

You may work individually or in small groups for this activity.

▶ Some events to cover for your school magazine.

1 Choose a suitable topic for your article. It may be a recent event like one shown in the photographs, or a similar one. At least **one** of the following conditions must be true:

▶ you saw the event yourself, or

▶ you can interview people who were there, or

▶ you have at least **two** different sources of information about it, such as a newspaper article and a report on television.

2 In your notebook, write down a list of points to be covered. Use the ones here as a guide.

3 Copy these points (or similar ones of your choice) into your notebook.

4 If you saw the event yourself, fill in brief details which cover the main points. Otherwise, interview the people who did see the event, or look at the reports of it, and fill the details in.

5 At the computer, start the word processing program and open up a new document for your report. Give the document a suitable name and make a note of it.

6 Type a headline for your report, and then some sub-headings for the main aspects of the story. Use the screen below as an example, but do **not** copy it.

Event:

Date:

Time:

Place:

Names of people involved:

Sequence of events:

Interview notes:

▶ A page of a notebook with the main points to be covered.

```
FIRE AT MIDNIGHT

How it started

The fire brigade arrives

Rescuing the children

Putting it out

Clearing up the mess

How the family are coping
```

▶ The headline and sub-headings for a magazine article.

7 Move the cursor to the first sub-heading, and start filling in the details. Keep it brief — no more then three or four sentences under each sub-heading. Write simply and clearly.

8 When you have finished, move the cursor to the start of the article and check it. Correct any spelling and grammar mistakes.

9 Save the first draft of the article on disk and print it.

10 Away from the computer, read the first draft carefully, making corrections and changes which you think will improve it.

11 Back at the computer, start the word processing program and call up your article. Make the changes you have marked on the first draft, and then check the final version carefully. Make sure that

you have corrected **all** the errors, and have not introduced any new ones.

12 Save the final version of your article on disk and print it.

ACTIVITY 2C *Topic Report*

This activity is best done by a group of three or four pupils. The aim is to select a topic of interest to the community, find out about it, make some suggestions about what should be done, and then prepare a report using word processing.

The photographs suggest some possible topics for the report: plans for a commnity centre, improvements to local roads, leisure interests of fellow pupils, dealing with pollution, the influence of television, or ways of making the neighbourhood safer at night. These are only suggestions, you may be able to think of a more suitable topic for your own group.

▶ The kinds of subject you might choose for your topic report.

15

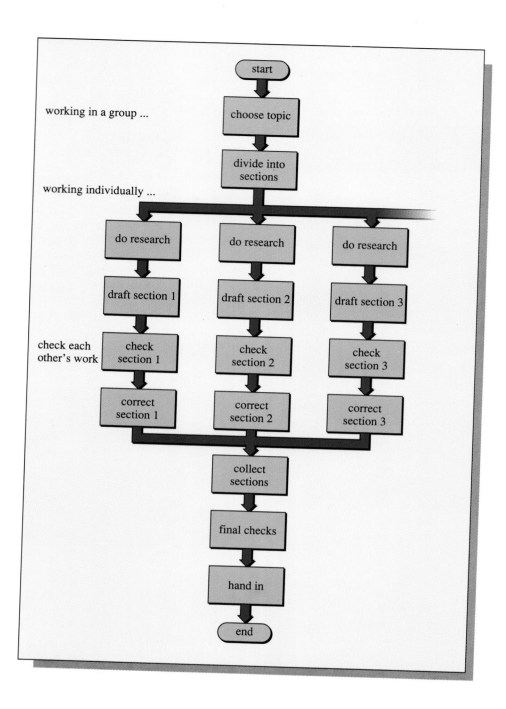

working in a group ...

working individually ...

check each
other's work

▶ Figure 2.1: A plan for preparing a
topic report.

There are a number of stages in the preparation of the report, and
it is likely to take several weeks. Figure 2.1 shows one way of going
about the work, but it is not the only possible method.

1 When your group has been formed, discuss the possible topics
   and select one. Make sure that it is different from those selected
   by other groups.

2 Draw up a plan for the preparation of your report, using Figure
   2.1 as a guide, but do **not** copy it. On your plan, write down
   which members of the group will do which parts of the work.
   Make a copy of the plan for each member of the group.

3 The next step is for each member of the group to do their research: talking to people, reading local newspapers, going and looking at the places concerned. Make notes of the information you gather in a notebook.

4 Each member of the group makes a first draft of his or her section(s) of the report. Use the word processing program for this, first entering the sub-headings or the main points, and then filling in the details.

5 Check the first drafts carefully, print a copy for yourself and one for each of the other members of the group.

6 Read everyone's first drafts carefully, mark any errors you find, and discuss them together. Decide what suggestions you can make from the reports, and who is to write these suggestions.

7 Each member of the group corrects his or her section of the report, making the changes agreed when you all discussed them. Then write the suggestions which arise from the sections of the report.

8 Check the corrected version of the report carefully, and print a final copy.

Making Pinehurst Town Centre Safer at Night

By Susan Green, Shinder Patel and Alan Ross

Form 5C

June 1989

Contents

1	Introduction	page	3
2	Old people at risk	page	4
3	Young people's fears	page	7
4	What the police say	page	11
5	Our suggestions for improvement	page	15

▶ The title and contents list of a completed report.

---

9 Collect all the sections together, and give them one last check before handing them in.

This method of working in a small group to prepare a report is often followed in businesses and other organisations. The drafts usually have to be changed to reflect the views of other members of the group. Word processing makes it easy to correct and alter the drafts, so that everyone in the group agrees with the final report.

IT FEATURE

Keyboard, Display Screen and Printer

The three parts of a computer which are particularly important for word processing are the **keyboard**, the **display screen** and the **printer**. This section tells you a little about each of these.

Keyboard

The keyboard is for typing text and numbers into the computer. Computer keyboards have the same layout as typewriter keyboards, with a few additional control keys. The keys for the letters have no obvious pattern. This is because early typewriters got jammed if people typed too fast, so the keys were aranged in an awkward pattern to slow typists down. This pattern, called the **qwerty** layout after the first few keys in the top row, has remained the same for more than 100 years. Although it is rather difficult to get used to, the advantage is that all computers and typewriters have the same layout of letter and number keys. The layout of control keys varies from one type of computer to another.

▶ A typical computer keyboard. The letters always have the same layout, but the control keys differ from one type of computer to another.

Display Screen

The display screen of a computer works in the same way as a television set. It can show text and pictures, called **graphics**. Some word processors show text in black against a white background, just like a printed page. Most display screens work in colour.

The letters and pictures are made up of fine dots on the screen. The finer the dots, the higher the **resolution** of the screen, and the clearer the picture.

▶ Most computers can display a combination of text and graphics.

Printer

A computer can be connected to different types of printer, depending on the work it does and the quality of the printing required. For word processing, there are three possibilities: a **dot matrix printer**, a **daisy wheel printer**, or a **laser printer**.

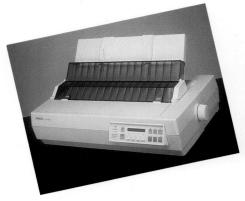

▶ Three popular types of printer — dot matrix, daisy wheel and laser printers.

A **dot matrix printer** forms characters as patterns of fine dots. It can print both text (in different sizes) and graphics. The pattern of the dots can be seen, giving the text a rather jagged appearance. Dot matrix printers are cheaper than other kinds, and are adequate for drafts of documents.

Daisy wheel printers have a rotating wheel which brings each letter to the print position. They can print text in one size only, and cannot print graphics. The quality of the printing is better than that produced by dot matrix printers, but they are more expensive (and somewhat noisy). Daisy wheel printers are most commonly used for business letters.

Laser printers use a laser beam to mark out the letters and graphics. A pattern of dots is used, but they are so small that they are hardly visible, and the quality of printing is high. Laser printers can print in a variety of text styles and sizes, and can form shades of grey in graphics. The speed of printing depends on what is being printed — a page of complex graphics is slow, but a page of text is quite quick. At present laser printers are a lot more expensive than daisy wheel printers, but they are getting cheaper all the time.

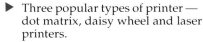

These automatic gates are controlled by microchips similar to those used in computers. It is an electronic control system.

These automatic gates are controlled by microchips similar to those used in computers. It is an electronic control system.

These automatic gates are controlled by microchips similar to those used in computers. It is an electronic control system.

▶ Examples of text from dot matrix, daisy wheel and laser printers.

| TOPIC | *Presenting Information* |

▶ A word processor in use in an office.

Word processing is all about putting information and ideas across, in written form, as clearly and effectively as possible. A word processor helps you to achieve this, but it does not do it for you!

To make the most of a word processor, you need to:

▶ Decide what points you want to make.

▶ Plan the structure of your text.

▶ Decide what style of writing is most suitable for the subject. For example, a letter of application for a job needs a different style from a news story.

▶ Make a first draft, perhaps in point form to start with. Write as clearly and simply as possible in the style that you have chosen, thinking of the person who is going to read your text.

▶ Print the draft, and check and revise the printed copy.

▶ Correct the text on the word processor, using your marked copy.

▶ Check the corrections carefully on the screen before printing the final version.

This is quite a long list, just for a piece of text. However, using this approach leads to written work of a very high standard. This type of approach is used in writing articles, and books, and in business for letters, reports, instruction manuals and advertisements. Planning a piece of writing can take longer than actually writing it!

EXERCISE 2

Questions

1 What are the advantages of a word processor over a typewriter? List as many as you can think of.

2 Which type of printer is most suited for:

(a) rough drafts of documents

(b) business letters

(c) magazine articles with large headings and illustrations?

3 (a) Why are the keys in a computer or typewriter keyboard in an awkward arrangement?

(b) Suggest some alternative ways of arranging the keys. For each alternative, give its advantages over the qwerty layout.

4 In what way does word processing help you to produce better documents?

5 Many newspapers use **news agencies** as one of their sources of information. The news agency sends reporters to events, and then sends their reports to the newspapers. These reports are generally brief and to the point, describing the main facts of the story in a few words. The newspapers then edit the reports into their own style, combining them with information from other sources.

(a) Choose a suitable news item (from the television or a newspaper, but do **not** copy the text from the newspaper).

(b) Using your word processor, prepare a brief report on the news item, in the style of a news agency.

(c) Make two copies of the report, on the word processor.

(d) Edit one copy into the style of a popular newspaper such as the *Sun* or the *Daily Mirror*.

(e) Edit the other copy into the style of a serious newspaper such as *The Times*.

(f) Print all three versions of the story, and discuss the differences in style.

Things to Find Out

1 Find out how word processors are used in some local businesses. Find out what the benefits have been from their introduction, and whether there have been any problems. Discuss your findings.

2 Find out some details about and the costs of a few popular word processing programs. Draw up a table of the prices, and the main features of each one. Decide which one you would prefer for your own use at home.

3 Find out how it is possible to send a document from one word processor to another without printing and re-typing it. Is this possible between any two word processors? Discuss your findings.

Things to Do

1 Use a word processor to produce one or more of the following letters. Follow the steps of Activity 2A.

   (a) a letter to a friend, describing a recent holiday you have had

   (b) a letter to a newspaper, making a suggestion from your topic report for an improvement to the local environment

   (c) a letter giving a reference for an (imaginary) friend of yours who has applied for a job.

2 Use a word processor to help you produce one or more of the following documents. Follow the steps of Activity 2B or 2C.

   (a) a poem

   (b) a translation from a passage of French, Spanish, German or Italian

   (c) a summary of a book you have read

   (d) a report of an event in a foreign country, such as an earthquake, rebellion, drought or famine. Get your information from newspapers, magazines, television and radio reports. (This is best done as a group activity.)

▶ Some events in faraway places — ideas for your topic report.

3 Question 5 in this exercise can be expanded into an activity for the whole class. Working in groups of between three and five pupils, one group acts as the news agency, and the others as reporters for different newspapers. Each newspaper group chooses an actual newspaper, and uses a copy of it to get an idea of its style of writing.

   The news agency group makes up a series of reports on real or imaginary news items, and prepares these on its word processor. These are then sent, either across the network or by copying disks, to the word processors of the other groups. Each of the other groups edits the agency reports into its own style, and produces the text of a copy of its newspaper.

   The original reports, and the newspaper texts produced from them, are all printed, and exchanged for discussion and comparison.

CHAPTER 3

Spreadsheets

A **spreadsheet** is a table of numbers (and other information) set out in rows and columns. The place for each entry in the table is called a **cell**. You create a spreadsheet by typing the numbers or words into the cells. You can change a number or a word in a cell simply by typing a new one in its place.

A cell can also contain a **formula**, so that the number in the cell is not typed in, but calculated from other numbers in the table. For example, a cell may have a formula which calculates the total of the column of numbers above it.

Once you have entered a spreadsheet, you can save it in disk. It is identified on disk by a name, so that it can be retrieved whenever you need it again. You can print the spreadsheet at any time.

Spreadsheets are set up by computer programs designed for the purpose. You do not have to know how they work, nor do any calculations yourself. All you have to do is make sure that the numbers and formulae are typed in correctly.

Spreadsheets are very popular in businesses, where they are used for recording sales figures, planning, stock control and invoices. They are particularly useful for trying out ideas and plans, to see what the consequences are.

	1	2	3	4	5	6
1	Weekly	Takings	18/03/89			
2						
3						
4						
5	Sunday 12/03/89	Total	Papers			
6	Monday 13/03/89	503.67	306.78	Sweets		
7	Tuesday 14/03/89	709.36	245.63	104.65	Other	
8	Wednsday 15/03/89	665.32	231.56	78.43	92.24	
9	Thursday 16/03/89	613.78	223.42	99.32	385.30	
10	Friday 17/03/89	658.41	248.91	83.54	334.44	
11	Saturday 18/03/89	727.51	252.63	86.32	306.82	
12		894.32	298.65	104.62	323.18	
13	Totals			132.67	370.26	
14		4772.37	1807.58		463.00	
15				689.55	2275.24	
16						

R12C3 = sum(R4C3:R10C3)

▶ A spreadsheet showing the weekly takings at a newsagent. The formula for the total weekly takings is shown at the bottom.

ACTIVITY 3A   *Weekly Weather Record*

```
1  ─────────1─────────2─────────3─────────4─────────5─────────6
2        Weekly  Weather  Record
3        ───     ────     ────              Week    18/03/89
4                                                   5       6
5                    Temp
6        Sunday      Deg C    Rain  Humidity  Pressure
7        Monday      8.3       mm      %
8        Tuesday     7.5       0                mb
9        Wednsday    8.1       8       53     1013
10       Thursday    8.9       11      72      985
11       Friday      9.4       2       78      964
12       Saturday    10.2      5       63      997
13                   11.6      0       71     1004
14       Average               0       67     1015
15                   9.1               58     1007
16                             4
                                       66
R14C2  =  sum(R6C2:R12C2)/7                          998
```

▶ Example spreadsheet of weather records. The formula for the average temperature is shown at the bottom.

In this activity you will use a spreadsheet to record weather information — temperature, rainfall, humidity and pressure — for a week, following the example above. You will calculate averages of these figures, and, if possible, produce a bar graph of them.

Before you start, make sure that you understand what these figures represent, and decide how you are going to obtain them. You have a number of options: a school weather station, if there is one, a local newspaper, or weather reports on the radio or television. You may also find local weather figures on a viewdata service (see Chapter 8). If you use the school weather station, make sure that you take the readings at the same time each day.

The first stage in the process is to set up the spreadsheet with all the information and formulae except the figures themselves. It is suggested that you work in groups of two or three.

1 Start the spreadsheet program running, and open up a new blank spreadsheet. Give it a name (to identify it on disk), and a title and date if you are asked for these.

2 You will find the top left cell **highlighted**, either with a bright rectangle or brackets around it. As you press the arrow keys (or move the mouse), the highlight moves from cell to cell. At the bottom of the spreadsheet, the position of the highlighted cell is indicated. It is either in row/column number format:

   R1C1   (for the top left cell)

or has a letter for the column and a number for the row:

A1   (also for the top left cell).

Whichever notation is used, you must follow it when you enter formulae.

3 Type the word 'Weekly' in the top left cell, and underline it with a row of minus signs in the second row.

4 Type the remaining headings in the top row, and the underlines in the second row.

5 Leave the third row blank, and type the measurement headings and units in the fourth and fifth rows.

6 Work your way down the first column, typing the days of the week, abbreviating them if necessary, to fit the column width.

7 Type the word 'Average' and the underlines in the 13th, 14th and 15th rows.

8 Move the highlight to the second column (temperatures) and set it to show numbers to one decimal place. Look up the method for this in the instructions for the spreadsheet program.

9 Move the highlight to the cell for the average temperature (cell R14C2 or B14, depending on your spreadsheet) and type the formula. In most spreadsheet programs, you start typing from the equals sign. The two alternative forms are shown below:

R14C2 = sum(R6C2:R12C2)/7   or

B14 = sum(B6:B12)/7

The formula is not shown in the cell itself, but it appears at the bottom of the screen when the cell is highlighted.

10 Work out the formulae for the remaining averages, and type them into the appropriate cells.

11 You now have the **grid** of a spreadsheet, which can be called up and filled in with weekly weather figures whenever you need it. Save your spreadsheet on disk and print it. Close down the spreadsheet program if no-one else needs to use it.

12 Collect the weather figures for a week, writing them in your notebook until you have them all.

13 At the computer, start up the spreadsheet program and call up your grid for the weather records. Change its name so that the filled-in spreadsheet does not over-write the grid version.

14 Move the highlight to the seventh column of the top row, and enter the date of the last day of the week you are recording.

15 Now fill in the figures you have recorded. In most spreadsheets, it is easiest to work down the columns.

16 If the spreadsheet is doing calculations as you type each number, you will see the average in each column change as you enter a new figure. Find out how to turn calculations on and off (on many spreadsheets you type an exclamation mark !). Turn calculations off if they are slowing you down, and on again when you have finished.

17 Move the highlight to the top left column, and then run it through the figures, checking them as you go.

18 When you are sure that all the figures are correct, save the spreadsheet (under a **different** name from the grid version), and print it.

Producing a Bar Graph from your Spreadsheet

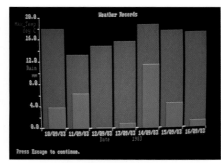

▶ The type of graph you may be able to produce from your spreadsheet.

If your spreadsheet program has facilities for producing graphs from the tables of numbers, or if you have a separate graphics program which can read the spreadsheets, then you can produce a number of graphs from your weather records.

It is best to use a **bar graph** to show the trends in the weather, and a **line graph** to see if there are any relationships between the figures (humidity and rainfall, for example).

For the first graph, produce a (vertical) bar graph of temperature and rainfall.

1 Start the graphics program running, or call up the graphics facilities on your spreadsheet.

2 Call up the spreadsheet of your weather records, entering the name you have given it.

3 Select Bar Graph (choose vertical bars if you have the choice) as the graph type.

4 Enter a title ('Temperature and Rainfall') and date for your graph, and a name to identify it on disk if you are asked for one.

5 Nominate column 1 (days) for the *x*-axis, and columns 2 (temperature) and 3 (rainfall) for the *y*-axis.

6 Display the graph, and note any trends in the figures.

7 Print the graph, and save the graph description on disk if you are able to do so.

Now repeat steps 3 to 7 to get a bar graph of humidity and pressure.

To see if there is any relationship between the figures, produce a line graph of humidity (*x*-axis) against rainfall (*y*-axis). The steps are as follows:

1 Select Line Graph as the graph type.

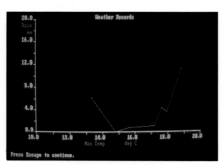

▶ A line graph showing the relationship between humidity and rainfall figures.

2 Enter a title ('Humidity against Rainfall') and date for your graph, and a name to identify it on disk if you are asked for one.

3 Nominate column 4 (humidity) as the *x*-axis and column 3 (rainfall) as the *y*-axis.

4 Display the graph. An overall slope indicates a trend in the figures. If yours shows a trend, decide what the trend is and make a note of it.

5 Print your graph, and save the graph description on disk if you are able to do so.

Repeat steps 1 to 5 to see if there is a relationship between pressure and rainfall.

ACTIVITY 3B | *Stock Control System*

A clothing wholesaler includes in its range three styles of T-shirts, known as **Ocean Mist**, **Banana Beach** and **Pacific Sunrise**. It receives orders for these from the shops it supplies, and orders large batches from the factory whenever stocks are running low. Records of the stock movements are kept on a spreadsheet.

```
          ___1___ ____2____ ___3___ ___4___ ___5___ ___6____ ___7___ ___8___ ___
                                    Month:   March    1989                      1
  1    Stock  Control                                                           2
       __         __                         __                                 3
  2                          Ocean   Mist   Banana   Beach  Pacific   Sunset    4
  3    Design:                        __          __                    __      5
                             In/Out In Stock In/Out In Stock In/Out In Stock    6
  4                          ____    ____   ____   ____     ____    ____         
  5     Date        Ref                                     661            1385  7
        ____        ____     ____    ____   ____            561     -250   1135  8
  6                                  485                                        
  7   01/03/89 Balances       -60    425    -100    801      240          1375  9
  8   03/03/89  Inv8923       240    665     240                               10
  9   04/03/89 Re-stock                                                        11
 10                                                                            12
 11                                                                            13
 12                                                                            14
 13                                                                            15
 14                                                                            16
 15
 16
          ___1___ ____2____ ___3___ ___4___ ___5___ ___6____ ___7___ ___8___ ___
       R8C4 = R7C4 + R8C3
```

▶ Example stock control spreadsheet. The formula for calculating a new stock level is shown at the bottom.

The aim of the stock control system is to record the number of each style of T-shirt issued whenever an order is made up, and the number received whenever new supplies come in. After each stock movement (issue or receipt) new stock levels are calculated for all items. This enables a continuous check to be kept on stock in hand. A new spreadsheet is used every month, with the balances carried over from the previous month in the first row.

Working in small groups, create a spreadsheet for this stock control system as follows:

1 Run your spreadsheet program and open up a blank spreadsheet. You will first create a **template** of the spreadsheet, containing all the information which does not change from month to month. This can be copied for each month's figures. Give this template a suitable name and title.

2 Enter the headings along the top six rows of the spreadsheet. Continue them rightwards to create columns for further products if you wish.

3 Enter a set of balances (stock levels carried over from the previous month) in the seventh row, and continue these across any additional columns you have set up.

4 Enter the Date, Reference and In/Out figures for the invoice and re-stock shown, again continuing them across the columns to the right. Note the minus signs for stock issued (you must enter these quantities as negative numbers), but do **not** enter the numbers in the In Stock columns.

5 The formula for each In Stock cell is the same:

Previous stock level (same column, previous row)

+ quantity in or out (same row, previous column).

For the first In Stock cell (row 8, column 4), this is:

$R8C4 = R7C4 + R8C3$ or

$D8 = D7 + C8$

Enter formulae following this pattern into the In Stock cells in rows 8 and 9, and switch calculation on to check the results.

6 Enter similar formulae into the In Stock columns of subsequent rows and columns so that your spreadsheet can hold at least **10** entries.

You may be able to copy the formulae from one cell to the next. Look at the instructions for your spreadsheet program to see if this is possible.

7 When you are satisfied that your spreadsheet is working properly, print it. Then delete the dates (including those in the first row), references, initial stock levels (in row 7) and In/Out numbers. Do not delete any of the formulae — when you re-calculate, all the In Stock figures should change to zero.

8 Save the template of the spreadsheet on disk. Give it a suitable name, if you have not already done so. Close down the spreadsheet program if no-one else wants to use it.

9 Away from the computer, write down a set of **eight** suitable invoice references and associated stock movements. Choose suitable starting levels, and plan **two** re-stocks to fill up depleted lines.

10 Start up the spreadsheet program again, and open the template of your stock control spreadsheet. Give it a new name which includes the year and the month to which it refers.

11 Enter the balances in the seventh row. Switch calculation on if it is not already on.

12 Working row by row, enter the information for each invoice and re-stock, using the figures you have written down. Note how the In Stock figures are filled in each time you enter a figure in an In/Out column.

13 When you have entered and checked all the information, save your spreadsheet on disk and print it. Make sure that it has a **different** name from the template.

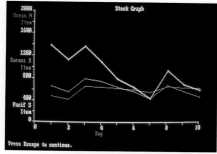

▶ A line graph of stock levels.

Producing a Graph of the Stock Levels

If you are able to produce graphs from your spreadsheet, it is useful to produce line graphs showing the stock levels.

1   Add an extra column to your spreadsheet, showing the day of the month only. This will be used as the *x*-axis of your graph. Copy the days from the dates column into this column.

2   Save the revised version of your spreadsheet, close down the spreadsheet program and run the graphics program.

3   Call up your spreadsheet, quoting its name.

4   Give your graph a title ('T-shirt Stock Levels') and a date if you are able to do so.

5   Nominate the days column as the x-axis, and the three columns of the stock levels (columns 4, 8 and 12) as the *y*-axis columns. Head them 'Date', 'Ocean Mist', 'Banana Beach' and 'Pacific Sunrise' respectively.

6   Display the graph, and note which of the designs is depleting most rapidly, and which least rapidly. (Is this easier to tell from your graph than from the columns of figures?)

7   Print your graph, and save your graph description on disk if you are able to do so.

8   From your graph, estimate suitable quantities to re-order if stock is re-supplied twice a month, and just enough is kept in stock so that the wholesaler does not run out before the new supplies come in.

ACTIVITY 3C

Exercise and Pulse Rate Experiment

▶ One way of taking your pulse.

The aim of this activity is to investigate the effect of exercise on pulse rate. Your **pulse rate** (the number of heartbeats per minute) is an indication of how fast oxygen is being supplied to your muscles. Exercise should make your muscles use more oxygen. This experiment gives you some idea of how much more is required.

This experiment is best done by a group of between five and ten pupils, each with pencil and paper, one of whom has a watch with a second hand. Before you start, make sure that you all know how to take your pulse!

1   Choose **one** of the following exercises to do. Make sure that you can do it without straining yourself, because you are going to repeat it a total of **40** times. It is preferable (but not essential) that all the members of the group choose the same exercise.

▶ Exercise 1: Arm Lifts: Starting with your arms at your sides and, keeping them straight, raise them above your head, and lower them again.

▶ Exercise 2: Sit Ups: Start by lying flat on your back, raise your body upright, keeping your legs bent, and reach with your arms towards your feet. Then lie back again.

▶ Exercise 3: Knee Bends: Start standing up straight with hands on hips, bend your knees, keeping your back straight, then straighten your knees. Keep your hands on your hips throughout.

2 Stand (suitably dressed) in an area with enough space to do your exercise. If you have recently been doing any exercise, pause until you have caught your breath.

3 Let one of you call out the start and end of a minute, while everyone takes his or her pulse. Write down the number of heartbeats you count.

4 Do your selected exercise at a steady rate a total of **five** times, all working together.

5 As soon as you have finished, take your pulse again for a minute, and write down the figure.

6 Repeat the exercise, this time **10** times. Keep a steady rate throughout, and work together.

7 Once again, as soon as you have finished, take your pulse again for a minute, and write down the figure.

8 Finally repeat the exercise **25** times, working all together at a steady rate.

9 As soon as you have finished, take your pulse again for a minute, and write down the figure.

10 Pause another minute, and then take your pulse again.

11 Have longer rest, until you feel that you have recovered, and take your pulse one more time, again for a minute. Write down this last figure, and compare it with the first one.

12 At the computer, start the spreadsheet program running, and create a new spreadsheet, giving it a name, title and date.

13 Enter the headings as shown in the example. Take turns to type your name and pulse rates in the appropriate columns. Check them carefully.

Exercise / Pulse Rate Experiment   Date: 28/03/89

Name		Pulse Rest	Rates 10 Times	Knee 20 Times	Bends 50 Times	1 Minute Recovery	Rest
Ann	Evans	75	78	83	102	85	78
Sue	Stephens	68	69	78	96	78	65
Clifford	Jackson	83	82	89	105	86	79
Colin	Trent	76	79	84	97	90	78
Andrew	McEwan	65	73	77	97	73	69
Winston	Mayall	85	88	93	106	98	82
Emma	Lee	91	93	103	112	100	87
Juan	Santos	68	70	78	96	80	69
Average		76	79	86	101	86	76

R15C3 = sum(R6C3:R13C3)/8

▶ Example spreadsheet of pulse rate experiment. The formula for the average pulse rate is shown at the bottom.

14 Enter the formulae for the averages, like the one shown in the example, and switch calculation on. Check that the averages seem reasonable.

15 When you are satisfied that all the figures and formulae are correct, save the spreadsheet on disk, and print a copy for each member of the group.

Questions

1 (a) At rest, who had the lowest and who had the highest pulse rates?

   (b) After the exercises, who had the lowest and highest rates?

   (c) Whose pulse rate reduced the most after the one minute recovery? (You may want to create an additional column in the spreadsheet to show all these differences.)

2 Did everyone's pulse rates increase after every set of exercises?

3 Comment on any differences between the initial and final pulse rates at rest.

4 Find out (from a PE or Biology teacher) how the figures in your spreadsheet can indicate how fit a person is. What conclusions can you draw from the answers to Questions 1 to 3?

Producing Bar Graphs from your Spreadsheet

The information you have recorded in your spreadsheet is a lot clearer if you can plot bar graphs of it. Use the graphics facilities of your spreadsheet program or a separate graphics program which reads spreadsheets.

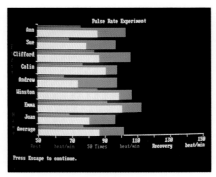

▶ Bar graphs from your pulse rate experiment.

1 Start the graphics program running and call up your spreadsheet.

2 Select a bar graph (horizontal bars if possible), and give your graph a name, title and date.

3 Nominate the headings row (row 4) as the *x*-axis, and the averages row (row 15), as well as the row for one of the pupils, as the *y*-axis columns.

4 Display the graph, and print it. The graph shows how the average pulse rate increases with the exercise, and the level to which it returns after some rest. It also compares the individual pupil's pulse rates with the average.

Repeat steps 3 and 4 for each member of the group, and possibly for pairs of members, if three quantities can be plotted on the *y*-axis.

IT FEATURE

Microprocessor

A spreadsheet is a convenient way of setting out tables of numbers so that the computer can do **calculations** on them. It is not the only way that calculations can be done on a computer — many computer applications include a certain amount of calculation. Calculating (sometimes called 'number crunching') was the original reason for developing computers.

Calculations and other types of information processing are done in a computer by the **processor**, in small computers the single-chip **microprocessor**.

The microprocessor chip is the smallest, fastest and often the cheapest part of a computer. It is made of a thin slice of silicon (the main ingredient of sand), approximately ten mm square. On the surface of the silicon are formed the electrical circuits which process the information. The silicon is treated in various ways, and is then coated with one or two thin layers of metal to form conducting paths. If the chip works correctly when it is tested after fabrication, it is likely to carry on for many years, without producing any errors.

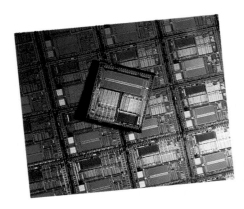

▶ A microprocessor chip, uncased, and an enlargement of the silicon portion inside the case.

TOPIC

Accuracy of Measurements

Numbers which have been produced by a computer look very convincing. They are neatly set out, well printed, and often backed up by graphs or maps. However, none of this is any guarantee that they are correct. The most famous recent example of a computer error was the failure of the Meteorological Office to forecast the hurricane which swept over Britain in October 1987, in spite of using one of the most powerful computers in the UK to produce their forecasts.

There are a number of ways in which a calculation by computer can go wrong. Several of them are illustrated in the last activity in this chapter. They include:

▶ Errors in taking the measurements which are put into the computer. For example, you could easily have made a mistake counting your pulse rate after one of the sets of exercises.

▶ Wrong calculations performed by the computer. It is possible that one of the formulae for calculating the average pulse rates has been entered wrongly.

▶ The variable nature of the information being measured. Your pulse rate does not remain quite steady, even when you are resting. If the same group of pupils repeated the same sequence of exercises and pulse readings another day, it is unlikely that the results would be the same.

It is important to bear these points in mind when looking at any set of numbers which have been calculated on a computer.

▶ Map of UK weather forecast, 15th October 1987. This weather forecast was produced by one of the most powerful computers in Britain, but it was wrong. It did not show the hurricane which was to sweep over the country only a few hours later.

EXERCISE 3

Questions

1 (a) How are cells identified in a spreadsheet?

   (b) What **three** things can a cell of a spreadsheet contain?

   (c) How are calculations done in a spreadsheet?

2 (a) From what substance are microchips made?

   (b) Is this substance rare?

3 List some of the benefits of using a spreadsheet to store figures and do calculations, over writing them on paper and using a calculator.

Things to Find Out

1 Find out some further uses of spreadsheets, in addition to those listed at the start of this chapter. For each application you identify, find out the advantages of using a spreadsheet over the previous way of doing the job.

2 Some computers have more than one processor. Find out how the processors in these computers are used, and what advantages they have over single-processor computers.

Things to Do

1 Use a spreadsheet similar to the one from Activity 3A to record weather figures over a longer period of time, say a month. Also include more weather information, such as wind speed and direction, and hours of sunshine.

2 Modify the spreadsheet in Activity 3B to keep the stock records for a school storage area, such as a textbook stock cupboard, or stationery cupboard. Decide what information to record instead of the invoice references.

3 Set up a spreadsheet similar to the one in Activity 3B to keep a record of the money in your bank, building society or Post Office account. Use one row for each transaction, with columns for the date, amount in, amount out and balance. When you pay in money, it is entered in the amount in column; when you withdraw money, it goes in the amount out column. The current balance is the previous balance plus any amount in minus any amount out. Use one spreadsheet for a month's transactions, where the first row shows the balance from the previous month.

4 Set up a spreadsheet of the world record times for a selection of athletic events. Use a column for each event, and a row for each year, or each time that a new record was established. Plot graphs from your spreadsheet showing how world record times have improved over the years. Why do you think they have improved?

5 If Activity 3C has been done by a number of groups, set up a spreadsheet to show the averages obtained by each group. Also include the number of pupils in each group. Calculate the **weighted average** of the groups, by multiplying each group's average by the number of pupils in the group, adding these products, and dividing by the total number in all the groups. Produce a set of bar graphs, showing each group's figures against the overall average.

6 A variation on Activity 3C is to set up an experiment to see whether people's pulse rates follow any kind of pattern in the way they vary during the day. Using a group of pupils, make a record of pulse rates at certain times of the day, for example: first thing in the morning before getting up, after breakfast, at morning break, after lunch, at the end of school, after supper and at bed time. Record all these figures in a spreadsheet, calculate the averages, and produce bar graphs to see if there is any overall pattern. If there is, try to explain it.

7 A spreadsheet can be used to store and analyse the results of a great number of physics, chemistry and biology experiments. Most experiments which produce a table of numbers are suitable. Calculations are often averages or similar operations, which can be entered as spreadsheet formulae without too much trouble. Graphs showing the trends in the numbers can be produced directly from the spreadsheets.

```
Client Insurance Policy Record

Surname:        Brown

First Names:    Susan Anne

Title:          Ms

Address:        13 Galway Road
                Wick
                Caithness

Postcode:       WY6 7GF

Policy No:      MVC7655498

Type:           Motor Vehicle Comprehensive

Date:           22nd July 1989

Status:         Active
```

▶ One record of a database held by an insurance company. It gives details of a client and the policy held by the client.

A **database** is a large store of information, set out in such a way that it is easy to keep up-to-date, and to find the information you want at any time. The information covers a particular topic, such as insurance policies in the example above. The items of information are grouped together: in the example above, all the items of information refer to the same insurance policy.

In most databases, the information is collected into **records**, such as the one above. A record contains a set of related information, for example all the information about one person, or one item (for a stock database), or one insurance policy (as in the example above). Each item of information in a record is known as a **field**. Examples of fields are the surname, first names and address in the example. The records in a database are usually arranged in some order. For example, the insurance policy records could be arranged in alphabetical order of surnames.

Databases are stored on magnetic disk, and a **database program** gives you access to the information on them. Most database programs allow you to create new records, delete ones you no longer need, alter the fields in records, sort the records in order, and find the records you want. Some have advanced features to combine records, count records, do calculations and create an index for quick access to the information.

Databases are used very widely in businesses, government departments, hospitals, colleges and an increasing number of schools. They have replaced filing systems which used paper records, with index cards to tell you where to look. These filing systems were slow and awkward to use, and easy to get out of order. Today many companies (particularly banks, building societies, insurance companies, holiday companies and mail order companies) rely heavily on their databases for most aspects of their business.

ACTIVITY 4A   *Equipment Inventory*

An **inventory** is a list of information about items of equipment (or furniture, paintings, etc.) which a person or organisation owns. It is a useful way of keeping track of things, and knowing how much to insure them for. If something goes wrong with a piece of equipment, looking up in the inventory can help you decide who to call out to fix it.

```
Item:                    Computer
Manufacturer:            Research Machines
Model:                   Nimbus PC2
Serial Number:           ABX18610110
Purchase Date:           25/01/84
Purchase Price:          1850.00
Maintenance:             MSM
```

▶ Example record from an inventory database. It shows all the information for one item of equipment.

In this activity, you will use a database program to set up a simple inventory, like the one above, and enter some records. You will then use the program to look up the records, and find out things from them. It is best to work in groups of two or three pupils. You can do an inventory of computer equipment, like the example above, or of other equipment in the school.

1 Start your database program running, and create a new database. Give it a name (to identify it on disk).

2 Enter the name for each field (Item, Manufacturer, etc.) and, if required, its width (the maximum number of characters which may be entered into it).

3 You may have to enter, for each field, whether it is a **number** or a **text** field. For a number field, you will have to enter the number of decimal places. All the fields of the inventory database are text, except the price, which is a number with two decimal places.

4 When you have entered the fields, check them carefully and correct any mistakes. Then save the record structure on disk. Give someone else a turn at the computer.

5 Find out the information you need for your inventory for **five** items of computer (or other) equipment (computers, printers, network servers, etc.) in the school.

▶ It is essential to keep up-to-date records of equipment like this.

6 Back at the computer, run the database program, and open up your inventory database.

7 Enter the information you have collected into five new records. Check what you have typed, and make corrections where necessary.

8 When you are satisfied that all the information is correct, save the records on disk.

9 Now use the **search** facilities of the database program to find information you want. For example, find the record(s) for the printer(s). To do this, you will have to issue a search command and then enter a **condition** something like this:

Item = Printer

Be careful with spelling and capital letters!

When you have entered the condition correctly, the first record for a printer is diplayed on the screen.

10 Make up conditions of your own, and enter them to see whether the records you want are found.

11 If your database program can add up totals, find out the total cost of all the equipment in your inventory.

12 Save the final form of your database on disk, and print it.

ACTIVITY 4B

Opinion Poll

Opinion polls are a systematic way of finding out what a group of people think about an issue. They are used very widely, on issues which range from politics to choice of washing powder. Computers are almost always used to store and analyse the results of opinion polls.

Types of pollution	Seriousness
Air:	2
Water:	3
Food:	5

Sources of pollution	Seriousness
Cars:	2
Lorries:	3
Factories:	4
Households:	1

Person answering	
Age:	15
Male/Female:	F

▶ A database record for an opinion poll on pollution. The person is asked how bad he or she considers each type of pollution is, and how bad each source of pollution is. Answers are numbers in the range 0 to 5, where 0 is not bad, and 5 is very bad.

▶ An opinion poll being taken in the street, and some results in a newspaper.

In this activity, you will carry out an opinion poll, either on the topic of pollution, like the example above, or on a topic of your own choice. Possible topics include television programmes watched and opinions on them, and community issues such as provision of youth clubs, care for old people, local employment opportunities, recreation facilities, etc.

You will design the questionnaire required, and, when you have asked the questions, you will record and analyse the results on a database. Work in groups of three to five pupils.

1 Decide on the topic for your opinion poll. Also decide whose opinion you want to investigate — that of other pupils, members of staff, parents of pupils, or another group.

2 Draw up a list of about **10** questions for your poll. The wording of questions is important — they must be clear, and must not suggest a particular answer. Phrase the questions as simply as possible, and ensure that they have definite answers (Yes or No, one of a fixed number of choices, or a number representing the level of agreement or disagreement). Include one or two questions which give information about the person answering the questionnaire (such as age or Male or Female, but do **not** identify them by name). Use the set of questions below as an example.

```
Pollution Survey
- - - - - - - -
How bad do you think each type of pollution is in this area?
Give a number from 0 to 5, where 0 is not bad at all, and 5 is
very bad.

Types of pollution
- - - - - - - - -          Seriousness
                           - - - - - -
1  Air:                      . . .
2  Water:                    . . .
3  Food:                     . . .

How bad do you think each of the following is as a source of
pollution in this area? Give a number from 0 to 5, where 0 is
not bad at all, and 5 is very bad.

Sources of pollution
- - - - - - - - - -        Seriousness
                           - - - - - -
4  Cars:                     . . .
5  Lorries:                  . . .
6  Factories:                . . .
7  Households:               . . .

Please give these details about yourself:

8  Age:                      . . .
9  Male/Female               . . .
```

▶ The wording and layout of a typical questionnaire.

3 Make a first draft of the wording of your questions on your word processor. Print this draft and check it carefully, making any corrections required. When you are satisfied with the wording, make a suitable number of copies (about 20).

4   Give the questionnaires to a suitable group of people to fill in, or ask the questions and fill in the forms yourself. Make sure that your group is **representative**. For example, if you want the opinion of the whole school, select about the same number of pupils from each year. Also make sure that the numbers of males and females surveyed are about the same.

5   When all the questionnaires have been completed, start up the database program, and create a database for the questionnaire. Set up a record for a reply, with a field for each question.

Use the record at the start of this section as an example. Do not worry if you cannot put headings in the record, as the fields for the questions are the important thing. All but one of the fields in the example are numbers.

When you are satisfied with the structure of the record, save it on disk.

6   Now enter the results of your questionnaire. Create a new record for each reply, and enter and check the replies. When all the results have been entered and checked, save them on disk.

7   For questions with numbers as answers, get the database program to add up the total of each of the numbers and divide by the number of records to get the average. This gives the average opinion for each question.

For Yes/No questions, and ones with similar answers, get the program to count the number of each. Convert these numbers to percentages of the total.

8   Write down the results. The best way of recording them permanently is to make a copy of the original questions using your word processor, and edit the copy to show the results.

9   Study your results carefully, and draw any conclusions from them. Write a brief report on your word processor, giving the results and your conclusions.

Additional Investigations

Depending on the nature of your questionnaire, and the capabilities of your database program, there may be a number of additional investigations you can make. For example:

1   Separate the Male and Female results, work out the averages for each, and compare them. If there are any differences which seem significant, try to explain these.

2   Group your results according to age, and again work out the averages for each group. Depending on the range of ages, use two or more age groups. Look for any trends in the results for the groups, and try to find reasons for them.

3   Either draw suitable graphs (bar charts are generally the best for survey results), or enter the results into a program which produces graphs and print them. Include the graphs in your report.

ACTIVITY 4C *Tourist Amenities Database*

When you go on holiday, it is important to find out about the area you are visiting. You can then choose the places you want to see, and check such things as when they will be open, how much they will cost, and how to get there.

In order to do this, information about the tourist amenities in an area needs to be collected, and stored in a convenient way. One way of doing this is to create a database of local amenities, which could be used by a local tourist information office.

```
Name:               Brentfield Water Mill

Type:               Restored Factory

Address:            Old Mill Lane
                    Brentfield
                    Middlesex
Postcode:           HA7 8UY

Telephone:          0435 768 231

Open Weekdays:      0900 to 1730
Open Saturdays:     0900 to 1800
Open Sundays:       1300 to 1800

Adult Fee:          1.25
Child Fee:          0.50
```

▶ An example of a record in a tourist amenities database.

▶ Some small tourist atttractions. To attract visitors, it is essential to get the right information to the right people.

In this activity, you will set up a database for the benefit of tourists visiting your area. It could be a general one, covering all types of amenities, or, if there are many tourist attractions in your area, you could select a type of amenity, such as restored buildings, or places suitable for young children. Work in groups of about five pupils.

1 Decide on the type of amenities for your database, and the area to be covered. If you are convinced that there are no tourist attractions in your own area, choose another area that you can find out about.

2 Collect information on about **20** places to be included in your database. There are several ways of doing this: looking at local newspapers and magazines, visiting the local tourist information bureau, if there is one, or even telephoning or visiting the places yourselves. Either write down the details about each place, or collect brochures. Make sure that the brochures give all the details you need.

3 Decide what information to include in the record for each amenity. Use the example at the start of this section to give you some ideas, but include more fields to cover things such as car parking, access by bus, coach or train, and facilities for disabled people.

4 Decide how to classify the places. You may want to set up a **code** for the types, to reduce the amount of typing.

5 When you have completed the design of the record for an amenity, start the database program running, and set up the record structure. Check it carefully and save it on disk.

6 Enter the information for each amenity. Check it and make corrections before saving it on disk. Print it for reference.

7 Test the database by entering some enquiries, and checking that the right amenities are located. For example, if your database includes museums, enter a query like:

   Type = Museum

Then check that the records for all the museums are found.

   Work out how to find out information such as which amenities are open on Sundays, and which can be reached by rail.

8 On your word processor, enter a set of instructions for someone else to use your database. Explain how to:

   enter a record for a new amenity

   alter an existing record

   delete a record

   print one or more records

   enter an enquiry, to find one or more records.

Do **not** assume that the person using the computer knows anything about databases. Make sure that the instructions are clear, and include the steps to follow if something goes wrong.

Check and print these instructions, and get someone to try them out who has not been involved in setting up your database. Revise and reprint the instructions if necessary.

Magnetic Disks

Magnetic disks store the information (as well as the programs) used by computers. They vary in size and capacity, according to the type of computer, but all can store large quantities of information. Some are **exchangeable** — they can be taken out of their disk drives when they are not being used. Others, known as **Winchester disks**, are fixed in their drives. The advantages of Winchester disks are their very high capacity and fast transfer rates.

Computers can read the information from any part of a disk at any time. Similarly, they can write to any part at any time. This makes finding the required data very fast. The information stored on a disk is permanent until it is overwritten by the computer. It does not matter if the computer is switched off or the disk taken from the drive. This makes magnetic disks so suitable for storing databases, as well as for many other applications.

Unfortunately, different types of computer have different ways of arranging data on disk. Thus a disk written to by one type of computer cannot always be relied on to be read by another type. Magnetic disks are, however, used to transport information and programs from one computer to another of the same type.

▶ A 3.5 inch disk, as used by many microcomputers.

▶ Exchangeable disk packs, as used by many mainframe computers.

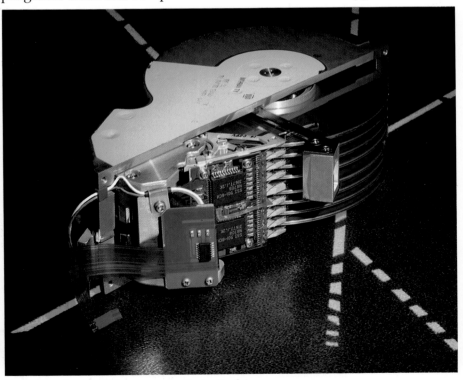

▶ A Winchester disk, permanently in its drive.

Personal Information on Computers

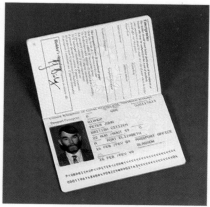

▶ New UK/EEC passports have a page of information which can be read by computer.

Databases are becoming increasingly common, and many of them store personal information — information which people would prefer to keep private. Information of this sort includes medical records, bank, credit card, building society and insurance company records, income tax and poll tax information and employment records. New UK/EEC passports have a computer-readable page, which could be used to record each time a person leaves and enters a country. Many people are concerned that all this personal information on computers might fall into the wrong hands.

In Britain, personal information stored on computers is controlled by the **Data Protection Act**. This requires all the organisations which hold this sort of data to be registered. When they register, they must state the purposes for which the data is to be used. Any use of personal data outside these registered uses is against the law. This means that, for example, a credit card company cannot tell anyone who enquires whether a person is behind with his or her payments. Any direct links for transferring information between computers which hold personal data are strictly forbidden.

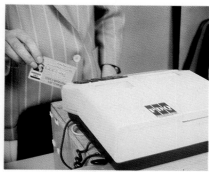

▶ A credit card being checked automatically by telephone. The magnetic stripe on the card allows the computer to locate the record for that credit card on the database.

▶ The 1984 UK Data Protection Act, which regulates the storage of personal information on computers. Similar legislation is in force in other European countries.

EXERCISE 4

Questions

1 Write down the meanings of the terms **record** and **field,** as they apply to databases.

2 In the introduction to this chapter, it is suggested that the insurance policy records are stored in alphabetical order of surnames.

(a) Suggest a disadvantage of storing records in this order.

(b) Suggest an alternative order for the records.

(c) How could a record be located quickly from the person's name, if they are not stored in alphabetical order of surnames?

3 List some applications of databases in:

(a) business

(b) education

(c) medicine

(d) science

(e) government.

4 Choose **one** application in each category in Question 3, and state what personal information is included in the database.

5 (a) Make a list of the topics of information about yourself which you would not like others to know about. These might include your age, what illnesses you have had, how much pocket money you get, etc.

(b) For each topic, write down the types of database on which it might be stored. For example, your age (or date of birth) might be stored on an insurance policy database.

(c) Compare your results with those of others, and discuss them.

Things to Do

1 Use a database program to set up a list of names and addresses. Decide what you will use the data for: members of a club, a list of your friends, or some other purpose. Then decide how you are going to record the information. For example, do you want to store first names and surnames separately, and how many lines of address do you need?

When you have planned the database, create it and enter a set of information.

2 There have been 56 monarchs in Britain from Alfred the Great to Elizabeth II. The list on page 45 gives their names and dates of accession.

Use this information as the basis of a database on the British monarchy. Find out additional information, such as date of birth, name of the husband or wife (or wives), how the monarch was replaced (died in office, deposed, killed, abdicated, etc.). Also find out the names of parents and children, and which of these were monarchs in their own right.

1	Alfred the Great	871	29	Henry V	1413
2	Edward the Elder	899	30	Henry VI	1422
3	Athelstan	924	31	Edward IV	1461
4	Edmund the Elder	939	32	Edward V	1483
5	Edred	946	33	Richard III	1483
6	Edwyn	955	34	Henry VII	1485
7	Edgar	959	35	Henry VIII	1509
8	Edward the Martyr	975	36	Edward VI	1547
9	Ethelred	979	37	Jane	1553
10	Edmund Ironside	1016	38	Mary I	1553
11	Canute	1016	39	Elizabeth I	1558
12	Harold I	1033	40	James I	1603
13	Hardicanute	1040	41	Charles I*	1625
14	Edward the Confessor	1042	42	Charles II	1660
15	Harold II	1066	43	James II	1685
16	William the Conqueror	1066	44	William III	1689
17	William II	1087	45	Anne	1702
18	Henry I	1100	46	George I	1714
19	Stephen	1135	47	George II	1727
20	Henry II	1154	48	George III	1760
21	Richard I	1189	49	George IV	1820
22	John	1199	50	William IV	1830
23	Henry III	1216	51	Victoria	1837
24	Edward I	1272	52	Edward VII	1901
25	Edward II	1307	53	George V	1910
26	Edward III	1327	54	Edward VIII	1936
27	Richard II	1377	55	George VI	1936
28	Henry IV	1399	56	Elizabeth II	1952

* Note that Britain had a civilian government under Oliver Cromwell from 1649 to 1660.

▶ The monarchs of Britain from Alfred the Great to Elizabeth II.

When you have completed your research, enter the information into a suitable database structure, with one record per monarch.

Use your database to find out information such as:

(a) the average length of a reign, both overall, and for kings and queens separately

(b) how many monarchs died in office, how many were killed, how many were deposed, and how many abdicated, and the names in each category

(c) how many monarchs succeeded one of their parents, and who they were

(d) how many monarchs were succeeded by one of their children, and who they were.

Try to find the reasons for the answers you get from your database, and write down your conclusions in a report.

▶ To get a balanced diet, the right mixture of different foods is essential. It helps to know the nutritional content of the food we eat.

3   In order to plan a healthy, balanced diet, it is essential to know the nutritional content of the foods we eat. A database is a convenient way of storing this information. The kinds of information you need to include about each type of food might include the following:

Name	
Protein	(g per 100 g of the food)
Fat	(g per 100 g of the food)
Carbohydrate	(g per 100 g of the food)
Water	(g per 100 g of the food)
Vitamins	(list)
Minerals	(list)
Energy	(kCal per 100 g of the food)
Notes	

The units given are only suggestions. You may find others more convenient.

Decide what fields of information to store in your diet database, and collect this information for about 25 different types of food. Enter this information using your database program.

You can use your database program to find out information such as lists of foods which contain particular vitamins, and ones which are rich in protein but low in fat.

4   The list below gives some further suggestions for databases which you could set up. Whether you choose one of these topics, or another of your own, the overall steps are the same:

(a) Decide the purpose of your database: who is to use it, what information it will store, and what they are likely to want from it.

(b) Decide the structure of a record in the database: what fields it will have, and the width and type of each field.

(c) Collect the information you need, or at least enough to start the database.

(d) Set up the record structure, and enter and save the first set of records.

(e) Use the database to answer the types of question you planned in step (a).

(f) Write a set of instructions for the use of the database by others.

(g) Collect additional information and enlarge the database to a useful size.

Suggested topics:

catalogue of your video, cassette, record or stamp collection; database of films, plays or television programmes you have seen; database of books you have read; field trip records: for geography or other field trips; motor car or aircraft database; database of recipes; results of a traffic survey; database of garden or indoor plants; database of birds, fish, wild animals or insects; inventory of household items; further questionnaires; holiday database.

CHAPTER 5 · Drawing & Animation

One of the most powerful ways of presenting information is by means of pictures. Written descriptions are greatly enhanced by well-chosen illustrations — drawings, diagrams, photographs, etc. Pictures are also important for their own sake: as works of art, as patterns on fabrics and as part of the design of many things.

Most modern computers have graphics facilities which enable them to display pictures in colour on the screen, and print them. Colour printers are available, which give a good impression of the image on the screen. Graphics programs enable you to draw pictures, save them on disk and alter them whenever you like. Some can take images from video cameras or scanners, and allow you to resize and crop the images on screen, colour them by hand, and combine them with your own drawings. Some programs enable you to produce sequences of drawings to create animation effects.

Images are displayed on a computer screen as patterns of fine dots called **pixels** (for picture elements). The closer together the dots (and therefore the more dots needed to cover the screen), the higher the **resolution** of the graphics. The higher the resolution, the clearer the picture. Dots are either in shades of grey or (more commonly) in a colour. Some graphics systems have a very large **palette** of colours, from which a smaller number can be chosen for each picture.

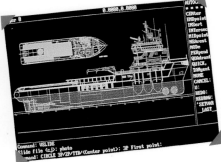

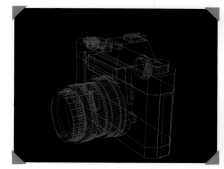

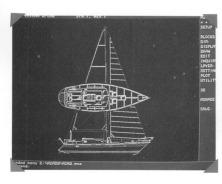

▶ A few of the types of image which can be produced on a computer graphics system. They include pictures drawn by hand, and images from a video camera which can then be edited and coloured by hand.

Computer graphics have many uses. These include the production of diagrams and cartoons for films and television. Animated cartoons produced by computer save many hours over the traditional process of drawing each image separately by hand. Newspapers use computer graphics to handle photographs and diagrams. Fabric designs are often produced on computer, as are sketches for designing clothes.

ACTIVITY 5A

News Illustration

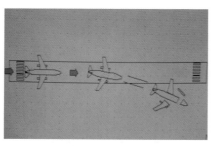

▶ When something like an air crash happens, there is seldom someone in the right place to take photographs as it happens. Simple drawings like this can be of great value in explaining what happened.

Much of the news we see on television or read about in newspapers is presented with the aid of photographs or film. However, some things happen too quickly for photographers or film crews to get there in time. These include robberies and disasters such as air, train and car crashes, and collisions between ships. In these situations, it is very useful to produce simple diagrams illustrating what happened. These are drawn from the information supplied by witnesses and survivors, and checked against other accounts, as well as the position of the wreckage, the nature of the damage, etc.

The aim of this activity is to select an incident of this kind, read some accounts of it, look at any photographs which are available, and then produce three or four simple diagrams (or one diagram showing several stages) to show what happened.

1 Work in groups of about three pupils, and let each group choose a recent incident to illustrate. Any event, whether local or national, may be suitable as long as there is enough information in the newspapers or on television about it.

2 Find out as much as you can about the event you are going to illustrate, and write down, in point form, the main steps of what occurred.

3 Decide how many diagrams to produce, and what to show in each.

4 Draw rough pencil sketches of each diagram, and check them against the information you have to ensure that they are accurate.

5 Run the drawing program on your school computer. Use a separate page (screen) for each diagram.

6 For each diagram, draw the main outlines first, then shade in areas, and fill in a few details. Finally add any text needed to label things.

7 Check each diagram carefully, and print it.

8 Write (or produce on the word processor) a few lines giving the date and location of the incident, and the main steps of what occurred.

ACTIVITY 5B *Illustrated Children's Story*

▶ Children's story books have a few words of text on each page, and simple, bold illustrations to go with them.

Story books for young children have a few short sentences, using simple words, and bright illustrations to show what is happening on each page. The aim is to make them interesting and fun to read. It's not as easy as it sounds!

The purpose of this activity is to produce a children's story, using the drawing program on your computer. The program should have sufficient text facilities to include the few words required on each page.

1　Working in groups of two to four pupils, first look at some children's story books to get ideas, and see what words young children are expected to know.

2　When you have decided on the age range for the readers of your story, invent one or two main characters and decide on a suitable event to form the basis of the story.

3　Now write the story, in no more than six short (but correct) sentences. Use simple words, but make it as interesting as possible in terms of these words.

4　Plan the page layout for your story. In most cases, each sentence occupies one page, although you may occasionally split one across two pages for extra effect. You may decide to have the text along the bottom of each page, or somewhere in the middle. The illustrations must fit into the overall design.

5　Draw (on paper) some rough sketches of the main characters, and the outline of the scene to be shown on each page.

6　Using the drawing program on your computer, enter the drawings for the first few pages. Draw the basic outlines first, and then shade in the coloured areas, and finally add a few details. Enter the text in its chosen position on each page, using an initial capital letter, and then lower case letters. Don't forget the full stop!

7　Save and print these first few pages, and check them carefully away from the computer while other groups have a turn.

8　Back at the computer, correct the first few pages, and then enter the rest, following the style of the first ones. In some cases, you may be able to save time by copying part of a drawing from one page to another.

9　Again save and print the pages, and check them away from the computer.

10 Make any final corrections before printing the finished version of your illustrated children's story.

11 If possible, try out your story on a child you know of the appropriate age, to see how well your ideas have worked in practice.

ACTIVITY 5C | *Textile Pattern*

The majority of textiles which are sold today have a pattern on them. The pattern is printed onto the textile in the final stages of manufacture, using special rollers with fine holes through which the dye flows. There is one roller for each colour in the pattern, and generally no more than five colours.

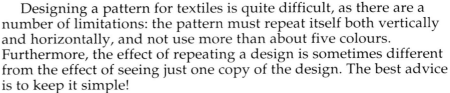

▶ A small sample of the types of design found on fabrics.

Designing a pattern for textiles is quite difficult, as there are a number of limitations: the pattern must repeat itself both vertically and horizontally, and not use more than about five colours. Furthermore, the effect of repeating a design is sometimes different from the effect of seeing just one copy of the design. The best advice is to keep it simple!

1   Working either individually or in small groups, look at some examples of textile patterns to get some ideas. There are a number of traditions to follow, and certain items such as flowers are used a lot. You do not have to follow a particular style, but a simple, striking design on a plain background is advisable for the first attempt.

2   First decide what type of textile to produce your pattern for. It may be for furniture, or for clothing — dresses, shirts and ties all have different needs.

3   When you have decided, choose an appropriate size for the pattern. You may choose a large design repeating (say) every 10 cm in each direction, or a smaller design repeating more often.

4   Then choose a **motif** for your pattern — flowers, waves, birds, ship's sails are popular, or you may select an abstract image. The motif is drawn once and then repeated vertically and horizontally to make up the pattern.

▶ A textile pattern produced on a computer.

5 On paper, lightly draw about four squares of the required size, and sketch the motif in one. Use no more than four colours. Repeat the sketch in an adjacent square. If you are very careful, you can connect from one motif to the next, but the link must repeat naturally.

6 Using the drawing program on your computer, set up a grid of squares on the screen of the appropriate size. (Make sure that you can turn these grid squares off, as they are **not** part of your final pattern.) If your pattern is too large for at least four repetitions on the screen, you will have to enter it half or quarter size.

7 Now draw one copy of the motif suitably positioned within the grid. Colour it using no more than four colours, one of which may be the background colour.

8 Save and print the single motif, and check it away from the computer.

9 Back at the computer, call up your drawing, and correct the motif if required.

10 Now make a copy of the motif (using the copy facilities of your drawing program), positioned in an adjacent grid square. Repeat the copying operation for each square on the screen. Be sure to position each motif correctly within its square.

11 When you are quite satisfied, save and print your textile pattern. If possible, print a number of copies, and then cut and paste them together to form a larger area of your pattern.

ACTIVITY 5D *Animated Cartoon*

A film or video captures the movement in a scene by taking a rapid sequence of photographs (known as **frames**), which are then played back at the same speed as they were taken. If you look at the individual frames, you will see that they show slight changes from one to another; our eyes smooth out these changes as we see the images in rapid succession.

The same effect can be produced by making a sequence of drawings, and showing them rapidly one after another. This is how animated cartoons are produced. To be completely lifelike, no less than 25 images are needed per second. Before computer graphics were used to produce these, they were all drawn by hand, using acetate shapes which were placed in position for each frame to be photographed.

These days computer graphics are used extensively for making cartoons. They speed up the process in a number of ways. Firstly, you can build up a library of pictures of the main characters in typical positions, and copy these into the frames as required. They are then altered slightly to fit into the scene. In a similar way, background shapes such as trees, houses, ships, cars, etc. can be

▶ Animated cartoon production in progress.

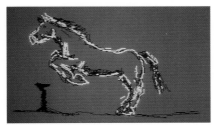

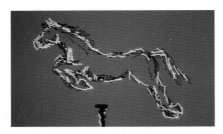

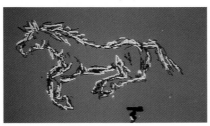

▶ To give the impression of movement, we need a sequence of similar drawings which are displayed on a screen quickly one after the other.

produced separately and copied when required. Secondly, some animation programs allow you to enter two frames, and will then automatically produce a number of frames with the in-between positions of the objects. Thirdly, these programs allow you to run through a sequence at various speeds to try it out, and alter the frames whenever you like. The large disk capacity of modern computers enables you to store long sequences of frames.

In this activity, you will first build up a library of pictures suitable for cartoon stories, and then produce a number of stories using these pictures. If possible, you will record a soundtrack on tape to be played while your cartoon is showing.

It is suggested that you work in groups of at least five pupils for this activity. Each group will produce a shared library of pictures. Then smaller groups or individual pupils will select pictures from this library to produce cartoon sequences. The cartoon sequences can be separate stories, or scenes from a single longer story.

1 Once you have formed the groups, decide on the theme for your cartoons, and the characters (people or animals) you will include. You may decide to build on the children's story from Activity 5B. One possibility is to let each member of the group be responsible for one character.

2 Draw some rough sketches of the characters, and discuss these within the group until you are happy with them.

3 Now run the drawing program on your computer (having made sure that it can feed images into the animation program), and enter about five sketches of each character. Show them from the front, sides and back, and perhaps in a running position. It is useful to make two or three copies of each drawing on the same page, and enlarge or reduce the copies to give a range of sizes of the same picture.

4 Then enter simple pictures of the scenery you will need for your stories — cars, ships, spacecraft, castles, etc. Again, make copies of different sizes as required.

5 While some members of the group are entering the characters, the others can be working out the plots for their cartoon stories. Keep them simple, and aim for between 30 and 50 images. If you show these at the rate of three or four per second, the effect is somewhat jerky, but it does give some sense of movement.

6 When all the pictures have been entered, print them and let everyone in the group check through them away from the computer. Mark up any changes which you feel are needed, and make these before starting on the cartoon sequences.

7 Working individually or in pairs, start on the cartoon sequences themselves. Start with a title frame, and then build up the first frame by calling up the pictures you need, copying them into your clipboard, and then pasting them into the frame.

8 Once you have pasted in the pictures you want, you can enlarge or reduce them as required, and alter then to suit the scene.

9 In a similar way, paste in any scenery you need. Finally, draw any additional items, and colour in the background areas.

10 Now go on to the next frame. You may find it easiest to make a copy of the previous frame, and then make slight changes to the pictures, or rub some out and replace them. On the other hand, you may prefer to build up each frame from scratch. It all depends on what is happening in your story.

11 Print and save each frame on disk as you go. You will probably have to give them names which form some kind of a series. Look in the instructions for your animation program to see what is required.

12 When you have saved all your pictures, check the prints away from the computer, and then return to it to make any corrections.

13 Now run the animation program, and load your sequence of images. Set the speed at which you want them to appear, and sit back and watch...

14 You will probably want to make some changes after the first showing. Use your drawing program to do this, and then run the animation program again. Also, adjust the speed until you get the best effect.

15 If the sequences produced by the smaller groups are scenes from a longer story, put them all together at this stage, and gather round and watch as the epic unfolds...

16 If you have access to a tape recorder (or can transfer your cartoon to video tape), devise a simple soundtrack for it. You will only have time for a few words or a short sequence of sounds for each individual scene.

   Use your imagination when choosing the source of the sounds, anything from milk bottles filled with different amounts of water to electronic synthesisers can be used.

   Run your cartoon while you record the sounds, and then play them back together. Make a few takes of the soundtrack, and then select the best one.

17 Finally run your complete story and soundtrack for the benefit of your classmates.

IT FEATURE

Mouse, Stylus and Image Scanner

Entering images into a computer requires input devices which are suited to the task. A keyboard is no use at all!

The commonest is a **mouse**. This is small, hand-held block which moves over a flat surface, and drags a **pointer** across the screen in accordance with the way it moves. This pointer can act as a pencil, paintbrush, spray gun or rubber when producing a drawing. A mouse is easy on the hand, but not very precise. It is hard to line things up accurately, and small movements can be difficult.

More accurate than a mouse is a **stylus**. It is like a pen and is held against a flat tablet. The position of the stylus on the tablet determines the position of a pointer on the screen. It feels like a fine pen to use, and movements can be much more precise than with a mouse. It is fairly easy to trace an outline with a stylus, something which is almost impossible with a mouse. The only disadvantage is cost; a stylus and tablet are expensive, and cannot be used for other purposes, unlike a mouse.

To capture an existing image, from a photograph or drawing, a video camera can be used. Better still is a **scanner** which looks rather like a photocopier, and gives a much higher resolution (and range of colours) than a video camera. Again, improved quality comes at a higher price.

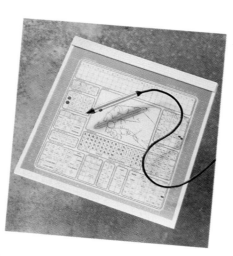

▶ Three ways of entering images into a computer - a mouse, a stylus and an image scanner.

TOPIC

Illustrations and Impact

▶ A typical page of a chemistry textbook from the 1950s, and one produced recently. The information is much the same, but the presentation is quite different.

Information which is presented only in written form can be dull and boring, even if it is full of important facts. Add a few well-chosen photographs, diagrams and drawings, and the same information has much more impact. The skill is in the overall design, the choice of photographs, and the drawing of the illustrations.

Diagrams are particularly important when giving instructions for doing something. They make the text much clearer, and mistakes are less likely. To see this for yourself, look at the instructions for operating something like a washing machine, or a first aid or car maintenance manual.

The design and layout of printed material — the combination of text and illustrations, use of colour, choice of typeface etc. — is a skilled job. The aim is to present the information in the most interesting and striking way. Magazines, newspapers, textbooks and technical manuals are all designed very carefully with this aim in mind. The success of the publication is often dependent on the quality of the overall design.

EXERCISE 5

▶ The design of a magazine is very important. It can determine whether the magazine succeeds or fails.

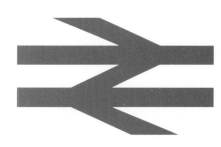

▶ The British Rail logo — identification without words.

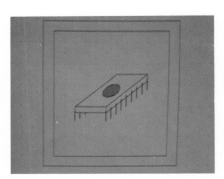

▶ A logo to identify classrooms and books used for IT within a school.

Questions

1 In what ways have the use of computers speeded up the production of animated cartoons?

2 What is meant by the resolution of a graphics screen, and why is it important?

3 What are the advantages of a stylus over a mouse for entering computer graphics?

4 List some advantages and disadvantages of doing drawings on a computer compared with doing them on paper.

5 What are the benefits of using illustrations as well as text in an instruction manual?

Things to Find Out

1 The input devices described in the IT Features are not the only ones used by graphics systems. Find out what others are used, and what their advantages and disadvantages are.

2 Find out what special output devices are used by some graphics systems.

Things to Do

1 Choose a page of an instruction manual which has photographs, diagrams or illustrations as well as text. Discuss the following questions:

(a) If you cover the photographs and diagrams and just read the text, do you still understand the instructions?

(b) If you had to carry out the instructions in a hurry, would you concentrate on the text or the diagrams?

(c) Can you see any ways in which the manual could be improved, either by changing the text, altering the diagrams or choosing better photographs?

2 A **logo** is a simple diagram which identifies something. Logos are used very widely, for example to identify companies, in traffic signs, or at places such as airports, to show people where to go. The benefit of a logo is that it does not need words. This is particularly useful at places like airports, where people from all over the world are in one place.

A useful exercise in drawing logos is to produce one for each subject taught at your school. You will need to think of a simple, striking image, which clearly identifies that subject. No two logos must be similar, to avoid any possible confusion between them. The logos could be used to mark the rooms where each subject is taught, the books used for each subject, as guides for parents' days, etc.

Discuss the image to use for each subject, and draw rough sketches on paper. Then use the drawing program on your computer to produce a set of subject logos. Print them, and test them out on other pupils, to see how many of them can identify the subjects.

3 Use the steps of one of the activities in this chapter, or plan the steps yourself, in order to produce any of the following drawings or designs on your computer:

(a) further news illustrations

(b) company logos (either choose an existing company and try to improve on its logo, or devise a company of your own)

(c) illustrations for a textbook

(d) illustrations for text you have produced on a word processor

(e) identikit portraits

(f) traditional art exercises such as a still life or perspective drawing (start with pencil sketches before you use the computer)

(g) sketches for fashion designs

(h) the design for the scenery and costumes for a school play

(i) a design for a T-shirt.

Work individually or in small groups as required. Some of the tasks benefit from a little research, particularly producing a good company logo.

4 If you have the necessary screen printing equipment, print the design you have produced in Activity 5C on suitable fabric.

▶ Some ideas for things to draw on your computer.

CHAPTER 6

Computer-Aided Design

Computer-aided design (CAD) is the use of computers instead of drawing boards to produce designs. CAD is used for all types of design: buildings, motor cars, aircraft, ships, and the components from which they are made. Silicon chips and computers are also designed on CAD systems.

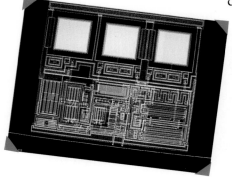

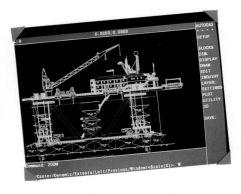

▶ Just a few of the many things which are designed with the aid of computers — the layout of a silicon chip, a building, and a mechanical part.

A CAD program is more than just a drawing program of the type used in the previous chapter. Each element in a drawing — line, arc of a circle, box, etc. — is handled separately, and can be moved, enlarged, reduced or shaded without interfering with the rest of the drawing. Any portion of a drawing can be selected and manipulated separately from the rest of the drawing.

Many CAD systems can work in three dimensions: drawings can be rotated to be seen from different views. Some CAD systems can be linked directly to machines such as lathes which produce the objects, so that the designs are made directly from the drawings. CAD systems for designing silicon chips include simulators which test the operation of the chip, and facilities which lay out the circuits on the silicon automatically.

A simple CAD system, of the type available in schools, has facilities which enable you to:

▶ Make drawings from lines, boxes, arcs and similar shapes, each of which can be manipulated without interfering with the rest of the drawing.

▶ Shade boxes and other areas, and move them one in front of another.

▶ Enlarge, reduce, stretch and shrink all or part of a drawing.

▶ Build up a library of items you are likely to use often, and paste these into drawings whenever required.

▶ Label drawings, and adjust the size of the text.

▶ Save drawings on disk, and call them up again when required.

▶ Print or plot drawings whenever necessary.

CAD systems are widely used in many types of industry. The aerospace industry — making aircraft and jet engines, and all the intricate components required for them — is heavily dependent on CAD. The motor vehicle industry is another major user of CAD. Civil engineering companies, which construct bridges, tunnels and large buildings, use CAD systems which incorporate many of the calculations needed to ensure the strength of the structures. The electronics industry makes increasing use of CAD in the design of silicon chips, printed circuit boards and complete electronic systems. Many architects are changing to CAD, particularly for large projects.

CAD has numerous benefits over designs on paper. The main one is the ability to modify designs easily. Designs can be revised as often as necessary, and new versions can be printed at any time. Libraries of common elements (such as the doors and windows of a building) can be built up, and copied into drawings when required, saving hours of repetitive draughting. The direct links with calculation, simulation and manufacturing systems also save hours of work, and ensure a higher quality of design than was previously possible.

ACTIVITY 6A *Process Diagram*

An excellent introduction to the use of a CAD program is to produce a simple diagram of how a process such as a central heating system works. The drawing is not a scale drawing of the equipment; its aim is to illustrate how it works as clearly as possible.

1 Working individually or in pairs, choose a suitable subject for your diagram. Choose something with which you are familiar. Possibilities are: the workings of a telephone, cassette recorder, refrigerator, or cooling system in a car engine; or a natural process such as the formation of rain clouds, lightning, oil or coal deposits, or continental drift.

2 Make a rough sketch of your diagram on paper, deciding what to include and what to leave out. Keep it simple, remember the aim is to show how something works, not to show in detail what it looks like.

3 Start the CAD program running on your school computer, and open up a blank drawing.

4 First experiment by drawing a few straight lines, boxes and circles, and finding out how to move them around, enlarge and reduce them, shade them in, make lines thicker and thinner, and delete them.

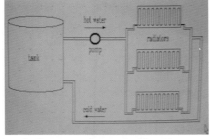

▶ A diagram of a central heating system produced on a CAD system.

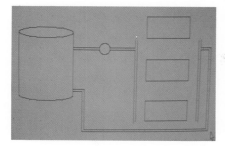

▶ The first stages of producing the diagram of a central heating system.

5 If the CAD program has a grid which appears on the screen, find out how to make objects stick to the grid points. Using the grid makes it easy to line things up, and get things vertical and horizontal where required.

6 Also find out how to group things together, so that they are moved, enlarged and reduced as one object. This saves a lot of time.

7 Now make a start on your process diagram. Draw the large shapes first, move them into the right positions, and enlarge or reduce them until you are satisfied.

8 Then add the smaller shapes and individual lines.

9 When you have all the shapes on the screen, experiment with different types of colouring or shading, to get the best effect. Do not overdo this, as it can clutter up the diagram.

10 Finally add any text, and move and re-size it if necessary.

11 Check your diagram carefully, save it on disk and print it.

12 Away from the computer, check the diagram and mark up any corrections which are needed. Ask yourself, 'Does this diagram clearly illustrate the process? Is there too much detail? Does the shading or colouring improve things, or does it confuse the diagram?' Alter your diagram accordingly.

13 Back at the computer, call up your process diagram and make the corrections. Check it carefully on the screen before saving and printing the final version.

ACTIVITY 6B   *Design a Container*

The container for a household substance must be strong enough to cope with all the handling, simple to construct and fill, easy to stack together, cheap to construct and attractive to purchasers. All these requirements make designing a container of this type much more of a challenge than it first appears. In the household goods industry, the design of a container can determine the success or failure of a product. A lot of time, effort and money is spent getting the packaging right.

The aim of this activity is to develop the design of a container for a household substance like fruit juice or washing powder. You will need to work out the measurements of the container, so that it holds the required amount, and draw the front, side, back and top views. You must also draw the unfolded view of the material (waterproof paper, cardboard, or plastic sheet) to show how it is cut out. In addition, you will need the artwork to be printed on the container. This can be drawn with your CAD program onto the views of the container, or with your drawing program on separate sheets if your CAD program is not suitable.

▶ A variety of household containers. They are all simple shapes, made from card, waterproof paper, sheet metal or plastic.

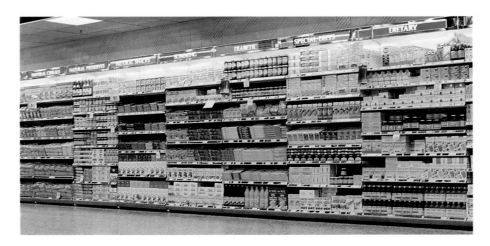

▶ In a supermarket, we are confronted with an array of packaged items. The ones we choose are greatly influenced by the packaging.

1 Working in groups of two or three pupils, choose a type of container, and a suitable volume (one litre makes calculations a little easier). Look at some examples of existing containers to get some ideas, but do not copy them.

2 Then select a shape for your container. The simplest is a box, but you may decide that a cylinder is more suitable. You may vary the shape slightly, for example having a 'roof' on the top of the box.

3 Work out the dimensions for your container. Decide whether you want it short and fat or tall and thin, and choose some dimensions which seem about right. Then use one of the following formulae (or one you have found out yourself for a more complex shape) to calculate the volume:

For a box: volume $= \text{length} \times \text{breadth} \times \text{height}$

For a cylinder: volume $= 3.14 \times \text{radius} \times \text{radius} \times \text{height}$
width of 'unrolled' circular part
$= 2 \times 3.14 \times \text{radius}$

It is suggested that you work in centimetres, remembering that one litre is 1000 cubic centimetres.

Once you know the volume from your first set of figures, adjust them and repeat the calculation, until you get the volume you require.

4 Run the CAD program on your computer, and draw the outlines of your container, viewed from the front, sides, back and top. (For a cylinder, draw one side view, twice the radius wide. Also draw an 'unrolled' view of the circular part, using the above formula.) If you cannot draw the views full size, choose a suitable scale. Check the dimensions and print the drawings.

5 On the prints of the drawings, make some pencil sketches of the artwork for the containers. Decide whether to emphasise the lettering, or to have a prominent picture. Also decide on colours; remember your container must be attractive and distinctive, and easily spotted on a supermarket shelf.

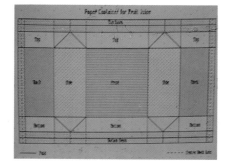

▶ A diagram of a container produced on a CAD system.

6 If necessary, decide whether your CAD program or drawing program is more suitable for the artwork.

7 If you are still using the CAD program, make a copy of your existing designs and enter the artwork — front, back, sides and top — onto the copy. This makes it easier to go back to the outlines if you are not happy with the artwork.

If your drawing program is more suitable, run it, and draw boxes of the approximate size of the sides of your package. Use the same scale as on your CAD program. Now enter the artwork for each side.

8 Print the artwork, and check it carefully. Look back at the requirements for a successful container at the start of this section, and decide whether your artwork meets them. Mark up any corrections.

9 Make the corrections to your artwork, and print two final copies.

10 Now work out the best way of making your container, if possible from a single sheet of material, by cutting and folding it. Decide how much overlap you need to make the joins. You may want additional areas, for example to form a spout when the container is opened.

11 Make a rough sketch of the sheet(s) to be cut out. Bear in mind the need to keep waste down when cuting out a large number of these sheets.

12 Returning to your CAD program, enter a drawing of the sheet(s) of material, either to the correct size, or to scale. Include all the overlap areas. Check the drawing carefully, and print two copies of it.

13 Now make up a paper model of your container, using one of the copies of the cutout plans you have printed. First paste the printed plan onto card. Then fold and paste the joints as carefully as you can. Cut out one set of the artwork, and paste it onto the model.

ACTIVITY 6C *Design a Room*

Whatever you do, at home or at work (or working at home), it is essential that the design of your working areas helps you as much as possible. Lighting, choice of colour and the layout of the working and storage areas makes all the difference. If you cannot see what you are doing, are too cramped, or cannot reach the things you need, you will never get anything done properly.

The aim of this activity is to design a room in which work is done, for example a kitchen or office/study at home, or a working area for one or two people at an office or workshop. The design is drawn as a **plan** (a view from above) of the room, showing the outline of the room, and the layout of the things in it.

The design is built up in two stages. First the furniture, lights and equipment for the room are entered into the CAD system, forming a **design library**. Then the outline of the room is entered, and different arrangements of objects in it are tried out until the best design is obtained.

▶ An office at home. Note the layout of the working and storage areas, how the lighting is arranged, and how the decoration relates to the use of the room.

It is best to work in fairly large groups when entering the design elements (furniture, lights and equipment), so that these can be shared among the group, and then in ones or twos to produce the actual designs.

1 Working initially in groups of five or six, decide what type of room to design. Look at some photographs and catalogues to help you make up your minds.

2 Next decide what furniture, lights and equipment to include in the room. Look at some catalogues for suppliers of this equipment, and note typical dimensions.

3 Choose a suitable scale for your drawings. It is best to draw the furniture, lights and equipment to a fairly large scale, and then reduce the drawings to match the scale of the room plan itself.

4 Share out the task of drawing the individual items amongst members of the group.

5 Start up the CAD program and enter the outlines of the furniture, lights and equipment, as viewed from above. Use the scale which you have chosen for the individual items. Do **not** include too much detail, but be sure that the measurements are realistic. Some objects like desks can be obtained in several sizes, so it might be useful to include drawings of more than one size.

6 If the item includes a door which opens on hinges, draw an arc of a circle in a suitable colour, to indicate the swing of the door as it opens. Similarly, for things like drawers which slide open, draw an outline of their position when open. This is to ensure that there is enough space for things to open when they are placed in the room.

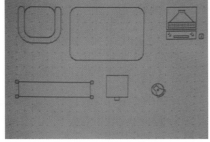

▶ Plans of some of the fittings for an office.

7 Save and print all the individual items.

8 Away from the computers, let everyone in the group check the designs of all the items. Discuss and mark up any corrections you agree on.

9 Returning to the computers, make the corrections that have been agreed on. Then make a copy of the final version of each design, and reduce it to the scale needed for the room plan.

10 Now form smaller groups (or work individually if there are enough computers) to do the room designs themselves.

11 First decide on the outline of the room, and the positions of doors and windows. You may choose a rectangular room to make things simple, but something like an attic room, or one with a bay window is more challenging. Use realistic dimensions, and remember that a large room does not necessarily lead to a better design, as things are too far away to reach or fetch easily.

12 Start up a new design using your CAD program, and enter the outline of the room to the appropriate scale. Plan the colour code for your design: possibly use one colour for walls, another for doors and windows, a third for furniture, and a fourth for the arcs of things opening.

13 Mark the positions of doors and windows, and draw arcs to show how these open.

14 Draw the outlines of any built-in furniture such as fitted shelves which depend on the shape of the room.

15 At this stage you may have to save your design on disk in order to open up the library of furniture, lights and equipment.

16 Now select from your library of furniture the main items to place in the room. Copy them from the design library (possibly via your clipboard) into your room design.

17 Open up your room design again, and place the main items roughly in position. Move them around until you get a good fit. Take into account the direction of the light from the windows, and the need to be able to reach the things you may want.

18 When the main items are in position, return to the library for the lights and equipment. Place these in suitable positions in your plan, and draw arcs around the lights to show the main illuminated areas.

19 Check your design carefully, and add a few details such as positions of plug sockets, the outline of a carpet or a few small circles to indicate plant pots.

20 Print a draft of your design, and check it carefully away from the computer. Try to imagine yourself working in the room, and think of any problems which its design might cause. Compare all the designs within the same group, and see how the same design elements have been used in different settings. Mark up any corrections you wish to make.

21 Return to the computer to make the final changes to your design, and print a copy of it.

▶ Plans of an office, using furniture, lights and equipment designed previously.

IT FEATURE

Plotters and CAD/CAM

CAD systems need an output device which can produce accurate pictures of the designs which have been entered and stored. These consist of large numbers of lines and shaded areas, possibly in different colours, and may be intended for large sheets of paper.

The most suitable special-purpose output device for these purposes is a **plotter**. It has one or more pens for drawing (one pen per colour). These are moved under the control of the computer to produce the lines and shading. The paper is either held stationary, or moves forwards and backwards while the pen moves from left to right. Plotting a complete drawing can take a few minutes.

The benefit of a plotter is that it produces a much more accurate picture than other types of general-purpose printers, few of which can handle large sheets of paper. The disadvantage is the high cost.

Some CAD systems not only produce their output in printed form, but can feed it directly into the machines which construct the things they have designed. This applies particularly to lathes, drills and other metalworking machines. The design controls the movement of the cutters and drilling bits as they shape the metal. This process is given the name **computer-aided design/computer-aided manufacture (CAD/CAM)**.

▶ A plotter in use printing a large design.

▶ Computer-controlled machinery in operation in a factory.

CAD/CAM has a number of advantages over previous methods: it is quick, eliminates errors between design and manufacture, and saves money as fewer people are needed to operate the lathes. CAD/CAM is widely used, particularly in industries which supply components for motor vehicles and aircraft.

EXERCISE 6

Questions

1. (a) How does a plotter operate?

   (b) Why are plotters particularly suited for use with CAD programs?

   (c) What is the disadvantage of installing a plotter?

2. (a) What are the benefits of CAD/CAM?

   (b) What adverse effect does a change to CAD/CAM have?

3. In which industries is CAD/CAM particularly common?

Things to Find Out

1. Find out whether any local companies are using CAD for their design work. If any are, find out what benefits it has brought over previous design methods. If any have rejected the use of CAD, or tried it and stopped using it, find out the reasons for this.

Things to Do

1. One of the most successful items which have been designed and marketed in recent years has been the personal cassette recorder. There are many variations now available. The main difference between them is their appearance, which is determined by the design of the plastic case.

   Look at a few different types of personal cassette recorder, measure them, and see what essential features they have (switches, sockets, ways of opening etc.). Then develop some ideas for a design of your own, which must be **different** from all the existing ones, and (at least in your view) more attractive to buy. Concentrate on the design of the case. Be sure that it is big enough to contain the cassette and the electronics, but do not concern yourself with the design of these.

   Use the steps of Activity 6B to enter your design, showing the front, sides, back, top and bottom of the case. Also show how it opens up to get cassettes in and out.

2. Use the steps of one of the activities from this chapter to produce designs for any of the following:

   (a) a simple object like the personal cassette recorder, for example a bicycle light, computer mouse, child's toy, camera, storage unit for records or cassettes

▶ Personal cassette recorders have become very popular in recent years. Now you have the chance to design one of your own.

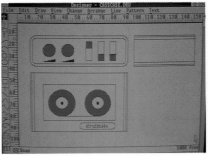

▶ A design for the case of a personal stereo system.

(b) a further process diagram, possibly for a simple industrial process such as making paper or purifying drinking water

(c) another container design, possibly for a more complex shape such as a shampoo bottle

(d) another room design, either for another room in a house, or for a larger working area such as a school computer room

(e) an illustration of a biological process like blood circulation or digestion (in the form of a process diagram, rather than a detailed sketch of actual organs)

(f) the plan of a town centre, recreation centre, marina or similar development

(g) the design, in outline only, of an aircraft, ship, car or train.

CHAPTER 7

Electronic Mail

▶ The post is too slow for many business communications.

F or several centuries the postal system was the most important means of communication for both business transactions and personal correspondence. The telephone has now replaced written comunications for many purposes, but there is still a need to send documents. This is particularly so in business, which depends on written contracts, orders, invoices, statements, cheques, etc. The problem is that the post is so slow. It can take days for local mail, and sometimes weeks for international mail. A business transaction between Europe and the Far East can be delayed by several weeks if documents travel by post.

For these reasons, links between computers are replacing the postal system for the sending and receiving of documents. Documents are prepared by word processor, spreadsheet or database and then sent via **electronic mail** directly from one computer to another. The computers on the electronic mail system are on a network, using central computers to switch the messages from the sender to the receiver. See Figure 7.1.

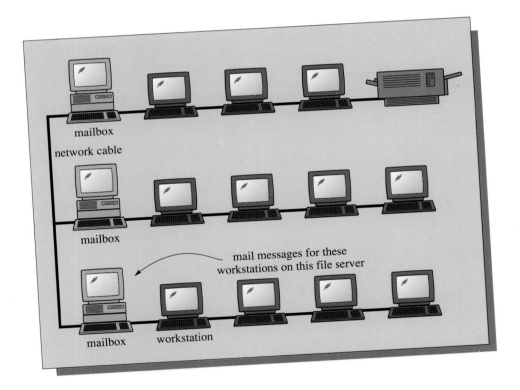

mailbox
network cable

mailbox

mail messages for these
workstations on this file server

mailbox   workstation

▶ Figure 7.1: An electronic mail system, showing the mailboxes to which messages are sent.

Electronic mail services can operate over wide area networks, or over local networks between the people in the same building. The way they work is the same in both cases. Each user on the electronic mail network has a **mailbox** (an area of magnetic disk) to which messages are sent. When you send a message, you address it to the mailbox of the organisation or person to whom it is being sent.

When you receive a message, you find it in your mailbox. You can then read it, or copy it to somewhere else on your computer, so that you can use the information in another program, such as your word processor or spreadsheet. Some electronic mail systems enable you to reply to messages as you receive them, and to forward messages to others.

Messages sent by electronic mail arrive almost instantly, and cost very little, in most cases far less than the cost of sending the same information on paper. These two advantages — speed and cost — are the main reasons for electronic mail taking over from the post for many types of communication. The main obstacle to the spread of electronic mail is that there are a number of separate networks in existence, rather than a single worldwide system such as the postal service. These separate networks are sometimes connected by **gateways**, but getting the right address through a gateway into another network gets rather complicated!

ACTIVITY 7A *Joint Magazine*

A school magazine with articles about your own school can be very interesting, but one with articles from other schools, possibly in other countries, is even more so. Activity 2B sets out the steps needed to produce a magazine article on your word processor; this activity extends the task to exchanging articles with one or more other schools via electronic mail.

A certain amount of planning is needed for this activity. First of all, contact needs to be made with another school which is willing to exchange magazine articles. If a group of schools can be involved, so much the better. Then test messages need to be sent between the schools, to make sure that their electronic mail systems are compatible, and that messages can be transferred to and from word processors at each end. Finally, the nature of the magazines need to be discussed, and suitable topics agreed for articles. These can be local news, sports reports, or articles on common themes such as pollution, job prospects, music, fashion, etc. Activity 2C gives more details.

If it is impossible to organise the electronic mail links between two or more schools, this activity can be set up between different classes or groups within the same school.

1 Divide into groups of two to four pupils. Each group will write an article and send it to the other school(s), and then receive an article from the other school, edit it and put it into their own school (or class) magazine. (This may also include articles from your own school.)

2 Decide on a topic for each article. Then follow the steps of Activity 2B or 2C to prepare, draft and correct the article.

3 When you are satisfied with the final draft of the article, use your electronic mail system to send it to the mailbox of the other school. Repeat the sending operation for each other school in the project.

4 Look in your school's mailbox, and select an incoming article for your group to edit for your school's magazine. Copy it from the mailbox into your word processor.

5 Read the article carefully before making any changes (you may not need to make any at all). Remember that your editing must not change the meaning of the article at all, even if you do not agree with it.

6 Decide whether the article is long enough for the space available in your magazine. If it is too long, carefully delete some of the details, and summarise where appropriate. If it is too short, try to find out more details and add them.

7 Correct any grammar and spelling mistakes, and simplify any parts which are difficult to understand. If necessary, break up long sentences, and replace long words by shorter ones which mean the same.

8 When you are quite satisfied, save the edited article on disk, and print it, ready to be pasted into the master copy of the school (or class) magazine.

ACTIVITY 7B *Orders and Invoices*

```
PURCHASE ORDER            From:  Sunshine Travel Limited
                                 8 High Street
                                 Ashbury
                                 Herefordshire   HE3 4RS

Reference: STL89097
14th August 1989

To Supplier:   Cosmos Computers Limited
               14 Bull Ring
               Birmingham B12 8UG


Please supply the following items, delivered to the above
address:                                                 Cost
Quantity Description              Cat. No.   Price        895.00
1        Astra Personal ComputerPC045       895.00       245.00
1        DSX Inkjet Printer       PR103      245.00        30.00
2        Box Printer Paper        PR563       15.00      - - - -
                                                         1170.00
                                                         - - - -
                                                          175.50
VAT at 15%                                               - - - -
                                                         1345.50
                                                         - - - -

Sharon Barnes
Finance Director
```

▶ Example of a purchase order, produced on a word processor.

▶ When components are purchased by motor car manufacturers, all the documents involved are exchanged by electronic mail.

When people at one company want to buy something from another company, they make out a **purchase order** for the goods. Using the other company's catalogue, they decide what they want, and the quantities required. They then fill in a purchase order form, giving the date, name and address of the supplier, and the details of the goods they require. The form also has the name and address of their company, and a reference number to identify it. An example of a purchase order is shown on page 69.

When the company which has received the purchase order supplies the goods, it sends an **invoice** with them. This shows the same information about the goods as the purchase order, but also includes other information such as delivery and insurance costs. The invoice states how much the company must pay for the goods, and when the money is to be paid. An example is shown on page 71, note that it includes the reference number of the purchase order.

In the past, purchase orders and invoices were exchanged on paper, even though they were often produced on a computer by each company. Today, it is becoming increasingly common to send these documents by electronic mail, saving time and money by all concerned. The aim of this activity is to try out this process of **electronic document interchange** or **EDI**, as it is called. EDI is particularly popular in the motor industry, for car manufacturers to order components.

In this activity, you will divide into groups, acting as purchasing companies and supplying companies. The supplying companies will draw up a catalogue of suitable goods, and the purchasing companies will decide what to order, and make out purchase orders. These will be sent by electronic mail to the suppliers, who will make out invoices to match, and return these to the supplying companies. If there are any queries, these must be dealt with via messages sent by electronic mail.

Before you start, make sure that you can send messages from one group of users to another over your school network, and that these messages can first be entered on your word processor. If you do not have an electronic mail system which can do this, work out a method of copying word processor documents to each other. This will act as your electronic mail system.

1   Divide into groups of two or three pupils, and decide which groups are to be suppliers, and which will be purchasers. The number of suppliers and purchasers should be approximately equal. Let each group choose a suitable company name and address, and a numbering scheme for purchase orders or invoices.

2   The suppliers each make out a catalogue of goods. These can be items of computer equipment, as in the above examples, or anything else which is suitable. Some suggestions are sports equipment, clothes, books or hi-fi equipment. A sensible maximum number of items in a catalogue is 20. These catalogues can be produced on a word processor, and a copy printed for each purchaser (or sent by electornic mail).

3   The purchasers examine the catalogues, and decide what to buy for their first purchase order. Use the one above as an example, select no more than five items, and remember to include the

VAT. Enter the purchase order at the word processor, and check it carefully.

4   The purchasers send the completed purchase orders by electronic mail to the suppliers.

5   The purchasers then start on another purchase order, to one of the other suppliers.

6   The suppliers, on receiving a purchase order, display it on screen, and check it carefully. If there are any errors, for example wrong or missing catalogue numbers, wrong prices, or incorrect totals, they send a message back to the purchaser, asking them to correct the error and send a revised purchase order.

7   If the purchase order is acceptable, the suppliers make out an invoice for the goods. Use the one below as an example, add a realistic amount for postage and packaging, and check all the figures carefully.

```
                                    Cosmos Computers Limited
      INVOICE                       14 Bull Ring
                                    Birmingham B12 8UG

      Reference:      435619
      Date:           24th August 1989

      Client:  Sunshine Travel Limited
               8 High Street
               Ashbury
               Herefordshire  HE3 4RS
      Purchase Order Reference: STL89097

                                          Cat No    Price      Cost
      Qty    Description                             895.00    895.00
      1      Astra Personal ComputerPC045            245.00    245.00
      1      DSX Inkjet Printer       PR103           15.00     30.00
      2      Box Printer Paper        PR563                     15.00
             Packaging and Delivery                          - - - -
                                                             1185.00
             Total excluding VAT                            - - - -
                                                              177.75
             VAT at 15%                                     - - - -
                                                             1362.75
             Total including VAT                           - - - -

      Terms: Payment within 30 days.
```

▶ Example of an invoice, produced on a word processor.

8   The suppliers send the completed invoices back to the purchasers.

9   The purchasers display each invoice on screen and check it very carefully against their original purchase order. If there are any errors, such as a missing or incorrect purchase order number, they send a message back to the supplier, querying the invoice, and asking for a corrected one to be issued.

10 Continue this process of electronic document interchange until each purchaser has sent at least one purchase order to each supplier, and each supplier has returned an acceptable invoice for all the goods which have been ordered.

Digital Telephone Networks

▶ A facsimile (fax) machine sending a document. An instant copy will be received by another fax machine somewhere else on the telephone network.

Electronic mail is only one of the many uses to which the telephone network is being put. As well as phone calls, the network carries **facsimile (fax)** messages, which are images of documents sent from one place to another. Links between computers carry large numbers of messages at high speeds.

The telephone systems in many countries are now becoming **digital** — the messages they carry are in the same form as the information in a computer. The exchanges which switch the messages from the sender to the receiver are **electronic**. They use microchips like those in computers, and are controlled by software like computers are.

These digital telephone networks and electronic exchanges can carry far more messages than older types of telephone system. They use the same cables to carry a variety of messages: voice, computer data, facsimile images, etc. The electronic exchanges can offer a range of new services. For example, they can store a computer message if the receiving computer is not ready for it, and re-route messages to alternative destinations. Once they are in operation, they are more reliable and cheaper to run than older types of telephone exchange. See Figure 7.2.

▶ An electronic telephone exchange, which uses computer technology to switch telephone calls and messages between computers.

The new telephone systems are known as **integrated service digital networks (ISDN)**. They are being linked by undersea fibre optics cables and communications satellites to form a worldwide digital communications system.

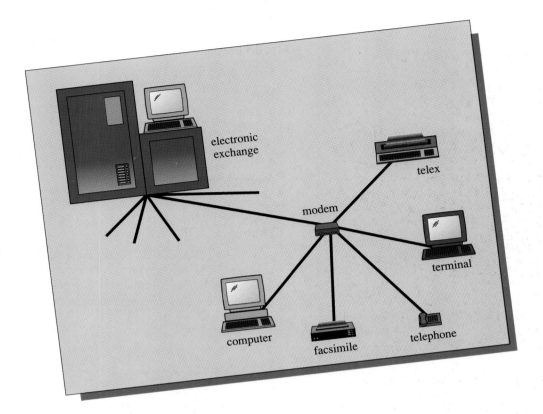

▶ Figure 7.2: Some of the services carried by the telephone network, and the electronic exchanges which connect the services.

EXERCISE 7

Questions

1 (a) In what two ways are computers similar to electronic telephone exchanges?

   (b) What are **two** of the benefits of electronic telephone exchanges?

2 In what ways are electronic mail and facsimile systems:

   (a) similar

   (b) different?

3 List as many services as you can which are provided by the telephone network.

4 What are the advantages of electronic mail over sending things by post? What are the disadvantages?

Things to Find Out

1 Find out as many uses of electronic mail as you can. Select one of these applications, and write a report on it. In your report, describe:

(a) what the electronic mail service is used for

(b) who uses it

(c) what advantages it has over previous methods of sending the information.

You may find it helpful to draw a diagram of the electronic mail network.

2 Find out what other uses are made of computer networks. List all the advantages they have over computers which are not connected together.

3 (a) Find out more about the way electronic document interchange (EDI) is used in the motor industry. What are the benefits of changing to EDI?

(b) Find out how EDI is being used in other areas (the UK National Health Service is beginning to use EDI, for example). In each case, find out what benefits it is bringing, and whether there have been any problems.

Things to Do

1 The steps of Activity 7A can be used for a variety of joint projects with other schools with which you can communicate by electronic mail. Some suggestions are:

(a) A chess tournament, with moves sent by electronic mail, and duplicate boards at either end.

(b) Linking individual pupils as electronic pen friends, and exchanging letters.

(c) A joint survey on a topic such as acid rain. The results can be collected on spreadsheets or databases, and these can be exchanged by electronic mail. All the information is then examined together, to look for overall trends.

► A screen of information from the British Telecom Prestel viewdata system. It is a public viewdata network, used in homes and businesses throughout the UK.

When you open a book, you see one or two pages of information at a time. You can read through the pages in order, or use the contents or index to go straight to the page you want. A **viewdata** computer system works in a similar way. When you use viewdata, you see a screenful of information (also called a **page**) at a time. You can go to the next page, or use the way the pages are organised to find out more information.

The information in a viewdata system is grouped in topics, with some pages giving lists of other pages which contain more details about each topic. For example, a weather forecast might have a map on one page, with the next page giving a list of the pages with detailed forecasts. Figure 8.1 shows how these pages are linked.

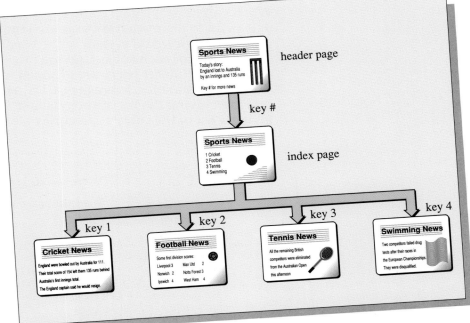

► Figure 8.1: Viewdata screens of sports news. Pressing a single key moves you from one screen to another.

When you are using a viewdata system, you press a single key on the keyboard (or the special viewdata control pad) to move from one page to the next. Only occasionally do you have to type the full page number to get to a page. This can be quite long, as some viewdata systems have thousands of pages.

The best-known viewdata system in the UK is **Prestel**, run by British Telecom. Prestel is received by a special television set or microcomputer connected to a telephone line. Prestel pages are supplied by a number of information providers, and cover news, weather, sport, forthcoming events, stock market prices, etc. British Telecom also operates a number of private viewdata networks, the

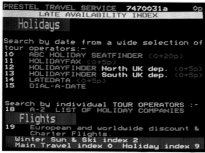

```
PRESTEL TRAVEL SERVICE  7470031a    0p
             LATE AVAILABILITY INDEX
   Holidays
Search by date from a wide selection of
tour operators:-
10   ABC HOLIDAY SEATFINDER   (0+20p)
11   HOLIDAYFAX            (0+5p)
12   HOLIDAYFINDER North UK dep.  (0+5p)
13   HOLIDAYFINDER South UK dep.  (0+5p)
14   LATEDATA             (0+5p)
15   DIAL-A-DATE

Search by individual TOUR OPERATORS :-
18   A-Z LIST OF HOLIDAY COMPANIES
   Flights
19   European and worldwide discount &
     Charter Flights.
  Winter Sun & Ski index 2
  Main Travel index 0  Holiday index 9
```

▶ The private viewdata system for travel agents displays details of thousands of holidays. It can be used as a gateway to the reservation systems for booking holidays.

most popular of which is used by travel agents for holiday information. The French national viewdata system is **Minitel**. It is very widely used, in particular because Minitel terminals are provided free of charge!

Although the idea behind viewdata comes from paging through a book, viewdata has a number of advantages over books. A viewdata system can store very large quantities of information. Prestel, for example, has tens of thousands of pages. Access to viewdata pages is quick, and the information is kept up-to-date all the time. Viewdata systems can be carried over long-distance networks, like Prestel and Minitel. Small, individual viewdata networks can also be set up, over a local network such as that in a school or office, or even on an individual computer. In this chapter, you will set up local viewdata networks for use within your school.

ACTIVITY 8A

School Subject Information

When parents or visitors come to your school, it is useful to be able to explain to them what subjects are taught, and how they are grouped. A viewdata system is one way of doing this. It has a screen page for each subject, giving brief details of what is taught in that subject. Subject pages are grouped into categories such as sciences, humanities, languages, CDT, etc. There is a page for each category, giving the list of subjects in it. There is also a header page, giving a list of the subject categories.

```
Subject:      Information Systems

Group:        CDT

Topics:       Popular computer applications, eg:

                  word processing
                  spreadsheets
                  databases
                  graphics
                  hypertext
                  desktop publising

              Case studies of computers in use

              Designing a computer system

              Effects of the use of computers
```

▶ A page from a school subject viewdata system.

When you use the viewdata system, you start at the header page, choose a category, and then a subject within that category. Figure 8.2 shows how the subject, category and header pages are linked.

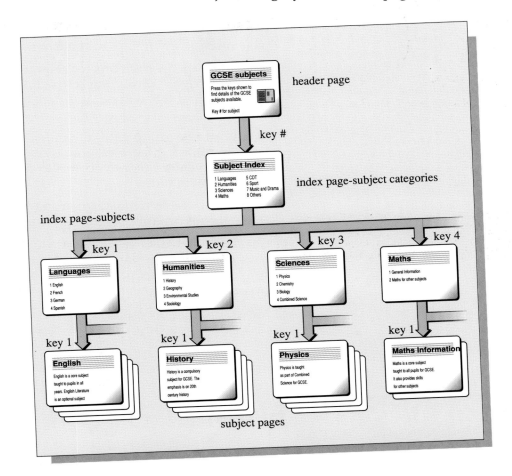

▶ Figure 8.2: Viewdata screens of school subject information.

The aim of this activity is to produce a viewdata system for the subjects taught at your school, either at GCSE (or equivalent) level or at A Level (or equivalent). One viewdata system is built up by the class as a whole, with groups providing pages for the subjects.

1 Decide which subjects you are going to include in your viewdata system, and choose suitable categories in which to group them.

2 Divide into groups of three or four pupils, one group per category if possible. Allocate a category of subjects to each group.

3 Within the group, allocate one or more subjects to each pupil.

4 Write a very brief description of each subject on paper. Use no more than 20 lines of no more than 40 characters per line. Include all the important points about the subject, but leave out all the details. Plan the best way of setting out the information, so that it can be read easily from the screen.

5 Start the viewdata system on your computer and take turns to enter the pages for your subjects. Pay careful attention to the layout of the information. You may use more than one colour, but too many colours looks confusing.

6 Check each page carefully, correct it, give it a name and save it on disk.

7 When all the pages have been entered and checked, enter the index page for the category, listing the subjects, and giving the key to press to call up the page for each one. Check and save this page on disk, giving it a suitable name.

8 Now enter the instructions for calling up the subject pages from the index page. Consult the instructions for your viewdata system to find the method; it differs from one viewdata program to another.

9 Finally let one group enter the index page for the system, which lists the subject categories, and gives the key to press to get each one. Again enter the instructions to call up the category pages from the main index page.

10 Create an attractive title page, using the viewdata graphics characters to produce suitable artwork.

11 Check the viewdata system as a whole. Start from the main index page, and work through each category and each subject. Make sure that the correct page appears each time you press a key. Make any corrections that are necessary.

12 Make sure that the entire set of viewdata pages is safely saved on disk before you close down the viewdata program.

ACTIVITY 8B *Human Organ Classification*

Each organ in the human body serves a particular purpose, but they can be grouped together according to their function. For example the respiratory system includes the nose, mouth, windpipe and lungs. Figure 8.3 illustrates the circulatory system.

One way of collecting brief details about organs in the human body is to produce a viewdata page for each one, and group the pages according to the function of the organs. A viewdata system like this allows you to look up the details of an organ quickly, and see in which group it belongs.

This activity can be done as a class project, with a group of pupils for each group of organs, and each individual pupil contributing the page(s) for one or two organs.

1 Make a list of the functional systems to be included in the viewdata system. Use a biology textbook or similar reference. Try to ensure that every organ of the body is included in one (and, if possible, only one) functional system.

2 Form groups of suitable sizes, and decide which group will cover each group of organs.

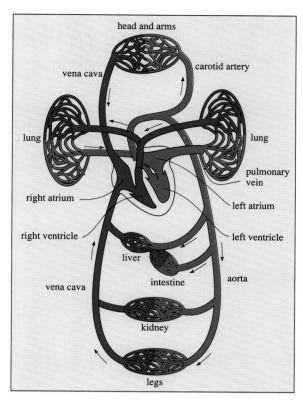

head and arms

vena cava

carotid artery

lung

lung

pulmonary vein

right atrium

left atrium

right ventricle

left ventricle

liver

vena cava

intestine

aorta

kidney

legs

▶ Figure 8.3: The human circulatory system.

3 Again using the biology textbook, each group first makes a list of the organs in its system. These are shared amongst group members for further investigation.

4 Decide what details to include for each organ. These might include:

the name of the organ
a brief statement of its function
its location in the body
its approximate dimensions and weight in an adult
any other organs to which it is connected.

Include sufficient information to fill a viewdata page, without it becoming confusing.

5 Each member of the group takes a turn to enter the viewdata page(s) for the organ(s) he or she has investigated.

6 All the members of the group then check all the pages entered by the group. Discuss their contents, try to 'even them out' if some are more detailed than others, and correct any errors.

7 When all the pages have been checked and corrected, one member of the group enters two header pages for the functional system. The first page gives the name of the system and explains briefly what the system as a whole does. The second page is an index page for the organs in the system.

8 One group enters a title page for the entire system, and an index page for the functional groups.

9 When all the information has been entered and checked, test the organ viewdata system as a whole.

ACTIVITY 8C   *Local Industry Information*

As traditional industries such as steel making and coal mining have closed down in many areas, they are being replaced by large numbers of small factories producing a great variety of goods. Many of these new factories are found in industrial parks, where the buildings are divided into a number of small units, each housing a factory or distribution centre. Some industrial parks are close to universities and polytechnics, so that the research done in them can easily be put to productive use.

▶ Industry parks provide small units for a variety of industries in one building or in one location.

It is useful to collect information about these small industries, and store it in a way which is readily accessible. A viewdata system is an ideal method. The information can be used to find out what types of goods are being produced in the local area, to investigate patterns in the location of industries, and when looking for a job. The aim of this activity is to set up a viewdata system for these purposes.

1   Working in groups of a suitable size (three to five pupils per group), first decide how to categorise the industries. You may decide to classify them by type of industry, or by location (for example take all the units in one business park together).

2   Decide what information to find out about each industry. Some suggestions are as follows:

> Name of company
> Address
> Type of product
> Number of employees
> Turnover last year
> Number of years established.

These are only suggestions. You may want to alter or add to them to make them more suited to your area.

3   Whichever way the industries are classified, allocate one or more classes to each group.

4 Find out the required information about the industries in your category. Use sources of information such as local business directories, local newspapers, parents who work for the companies, etc.

5 Run the viewdata system on your school computer and enter the information, one screen page per company. Set out the information as clearly as possible, and use the available colours with care.

6 When all the groups have entered their information, set up the pages for the categories, and the overall header page. Link up all the pages using suitable keys to go from one page to another.

7 Write a brief set of instructions for the use of the local industry viewdata system. Explain the purposes of the system, give the steps needed to get started, and look at various pages.

Questions

Look at the local industry viewdata information collected by the whole class, and try to answer the following questions from it:

1 Is there any obvious pattern in the location of the different types of factory? If so, suggest some reasons for it.

2 Are there any factors influencing the location of the industries? For example, are any industries which need large amounts of water located close to a river? Are ones which need to deliver large quantities of goods near major roads? Make a list of all the factors of this nature you find.

3 How many of the local industries trade with each other? Describe and comment on any local trading patterns you find.

IT FEATURE *Modem*

▶ A modem linking a microcomputer to a telephone line.

Public viewdata systems such as Prestel and Minitel use telephone lines to link the central computers, which store the information, to the microcomputers or viewdata terminals, where it is used. In order to link the computers to the telephone lines, a device called a **modem** (short for **modulator/demodulator**) is used. It converts outgoing signals from the way in which they are represented inside a computer to pulses which can be carried over a telephone line. Incoming signals are converted from these pulses into a computer form. Modems can operate at different rates, the commonest being 1200 or 2400 bits (binary digits) per second.

The direct links between computers and telephones provided by modems makes a number of applications possible, viewdata and electronic mail being just two. This combination of computing and communications helps to get information to the places where it is needed quickly and cheaply.

EXERCISE 8

Questions

1 (a) In what ways are viewdata systems similar to books?

   (b) In what ways do they differ?

2 What is the function of a modem?

3 Write down the names of some public viewdata services.

4 List some of the uses for viewdata system in business.

5 List as many activities as you can which are made possbile by direct links between computers and the telephone network.

Things to Find Out

1 The French national viewdata service, Minitel, has more facilities than its UK counterpart, Prestel. For example, it provides a reply service, where you fill in a form on the screen and send it back to the information provider, to order goods or request further information. It also has games, where you answer questions or decide your next move, and the next screen displayed depends on what you have chosen.

   (a) Find out more about these additional services provided by Minitel.

   (b) Find out how they are being used, and what effects they are having.

2 Find out if any local travel agents use viewdata for holiday bookings. If so, find out what the advantages of using the viewdata system are, and whether there have been any problems using it.

Things to Do

1 Use the steps of Activity 8A, 8B or 8C to set up a viewdata system for any of the following:

   (a) film information for a multi-screen cinema

   (b) an information base of local amenities

   (c) a local entertainments guide: what's on at the local theatres, cinemas, youth clubs, discos, sports clubs, etc.

   (d) information for school sports day, parents' evening, or similar event.

   (e) a football league information base: list the clubs in each division, the team members in each club, and have a page for each team member, with a few details. You might also include a results table for each division.

2   Use a sequence of viewdata pages for a simple cartoon story. Enter a few lines of text on each page, and a simple drawing in viewdata graphics symbols. Possibly make the story 'branch' to alternative pages depending on an answer by the reader to a question in the text.

Start by planning your story on paper, drawing a diagram of the paths through the pages. Draw a rough sketch of each page, including the text, before you start entering the pages at the computer. Limit the story to about 20 pages.

3   The structure of a set of viewdata pages is the same as that of a family tree. There is one page for each person, with links from parents to children. Choose a suitable family tree, either your own, or part of the British Royal Family (Figure 8.4), or a prominent local family (possibly one which lived in a nearby stately home). Find out a little about each person in the family, and enter a page for each one. Link the pages so that you go up and down the generations.

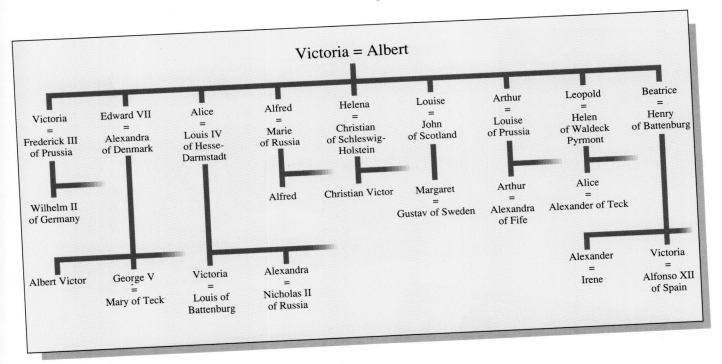

▶ Figure 8.4: The children and grandchildren of Queen Victoria — one possibility for a family tree viewdata system.

CHAPTER 9

Control & Monitoring

When you go into a station on the London Underground, you put your ticket in a slot beside the entry gate. The control system for the gate reads the magnetic strip on your ticket. If the ticket is valid, the gate opens; if not, a message is displayed. This system works without anyone operating it — it is **automatic**.

These automatic gates are controlled by microchips similar to those used in computers. It is an **electronic** control system. Microchips, specially designed for the purpose, are used in many similar control systems, such as those in ships and aircraft, cash terminals at banks, many industrial processes, and the road traffic control systems in some towns. Electronic control systems are also used in many devices in the home.

▶ Automatic control is used in many places, and most automatic control systems are electronic.

Control Signals and Gates

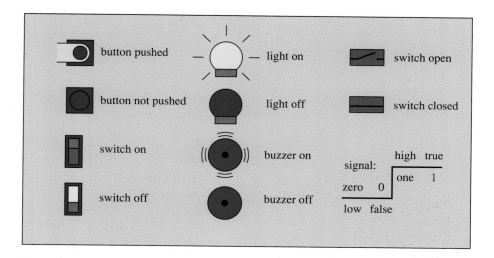

▶ Figure 9.1: Control signals.

The signals in electronic control systems normally have only two possible **states**. These can mean on or off, or true or false, or high or low, depending on the purpose of the signal. The states are normally indicated by the two digits, 0 and 1. See Figure 9.1. The reason for having only two states has to do with the way the electronic components work, but it simplifies the design of electronic control systems a great deal.

These signals are combined in an electronic control system by going through **gates**. The three commonest gates are NOT, AND and OR gates (Figures 9.2 to 9.4). The operation of each of these is described by a **truth table**, which shows how the signal coming out of the gate (the **output**) is related to the ones going into the gate (the **inputs**).

NOT Gate

Truth Table

Input a	Output b
0	1
1	0

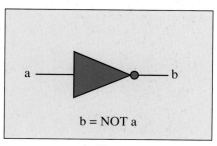

b = NOT a

▶ Figure 9.2: NOT gate.

The NOT gate reverses the input signal.

AND Gate

Truth Table

Inputs		Output
a	b	c
0	0	0
0	1	0
1	0	0
1	1	1

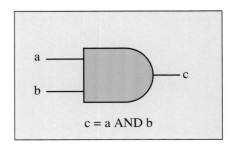

▶ Figure 9.3: AND gate.

The output is 1 if one input AND the other input are both 1.

OR Gate

Truth Table

Inputs		Output
a	b	c
0	0	0
0	1	1
1	0	1
1	1	1

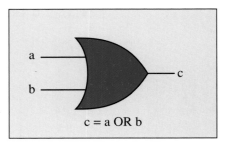

▶ Figure 9.4: OR gate.

The output is 1 if one input OR the other input is 1.

Counter

As well as gates such as AND, OR and NOT, one of the most useful parts in an electronic control system is a **counter**. It has two inputs, one to reset it to zero, and the other for it to count up 1. The number of outputs varies, but together they form a binary (base two) number. A four-output (or four-bit) counter is shown in Figure 9.5.

The count is zero if the reset signal is 1, otherwise it increases by 1 every time the count input changes from 0 to 1. When it reaches the limit of its counting range (binary 1111 or decimal 15 for a four-bit counter) it starts again from zero. This is shown in the table below. The table also shows the hexadecimal (base sixteen) and decimal output values.

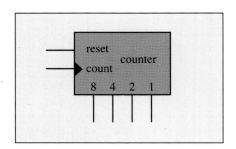

▶ Figure 9.5: Four-bit counter.

Truth Table

Inputs		Outputs—from previous number to:		
reset	count	8 4 2 1	hexadecimal	decimal
1	0 or 1	0 0 0 0	0	0
0	0 to 1	0 0 0 1	1	1
0	0 to 1	0 0 1 0	2	2
0	0 to 1	0 0 1 1	3	3
0	0 to 1	0 1 0 0	4	4
0	0 to 1	0 1 0 1	5	5
0	0 to 1	0 1 1 0	6	6
0	0 to 1	0 1 1 1	7	7
0	0 to 1	1 0 0 0	8	8
0	0 to 1	1 0 0 1	9	9
0	0 to 1	1 0 1 0	A	10
0	0 to 1	1 0 1 1	B	11
0	0 to 1	1 1 0 0	C	12
0	0 to 1	1 1 0 1	D	13
0	0 to 1	1 1 1 0	E	14
0	0 to 1	1 1 1 1	F	15
0	0 to 1	0 0 0 0	0	0

Counters, gates and similar elements are combined into **logic circuits,** where the outputs of some of the gates are connected to the inputs of others. The logic circuits for electronic control systems use thousands of gates and counters like these, as well as other parts for tasks such as storing information. All these are circuits built into a few microchips. In some cases, the entire logic circuit is built into a single microchip.

To make it possible for you to build simple control systems, **electronics kits** have these gates and counters as separate parts, which you connect with wires to form logic circuits. They also have a range of input devices such as switches and light and heat sensors, and output devices like lights and buzzers, as well as relay switches for electric motors. (A relay switch is one where a small signal opens or closes a switch which can carry a large current.)

Questions

1 (a) If one input to an AND gate is 0, what is the output?

(b) If one input to an AND gate is 1, how does the output relate to the other input?

(c) If one input to an OR gate is 1, what is the output?

(d) If one input to an OR gate is 0, how does the output relate to the other input?

2 (a) to (c) Write down the truth table for each of the logic circuits in Figure 9.6 on page 88.

3 Using Question 2(c) as a guide, draw up a logic circuit using three NOT gates and an OR gate, which has the same truth table as an AND gate.

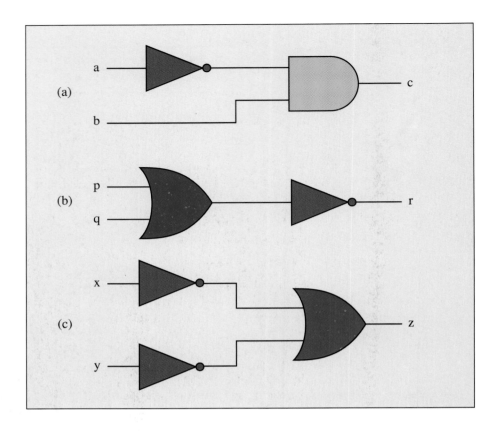

▶ Figure 9.6: Logic circuits.

▶ This car is protected by a burglar alarm!

ACTIVITY 9A *Car Burglar Alarm*

Many cars are protected by burglar alarms, which are set off automatically when someone tries to break into the car. In this activity, you will use an electronics kit to construct the logic circuit for a simple car alarm.

Your alarm has a main switch, and a pressure switch which could go inside the car door. The alarm goes off if the main switch is on, and the pressure switch is off (indicating that the door has been opened). A diagram of this circuit is shown in Figure 9.7.

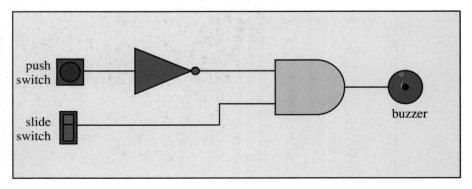

▶ Figure 9.7: Car burglar alarm circuit.

▶ An electronics kit connected as a car burglar alarm.

Connect the battery of your electronics kit and make sure that it is working. Then:

1 Choose a slide switch for the main switch, and a pressure switch for the other one. Connect up the two switches, the NOT and AND gates and the buzzer to make this circuit. If necessary, use the photograph to help.

2 Turn the main switch off, and try both positions of the pressure switch. Check that the buzzer does not sound.

3 Turn the main switch on, and try both positions of the pressure switch. The buzzer should sound when the pressure switch is up (released).

4 Copy and complete the truth table for the car alarm circuit.

Inputs		Output
Main switch	Pressure switch	Buzzer
0	0	...
0	1	...
1	0	...
1	1	...

5 Modify the circuit to include a light which goes on when the buzzer sounds.

ACTIVITY 9B

Pedestrian Crossing Controller

When you use a pedestrian crossing, you press a button to start it. There is a pause while the traffic lights go amber and then red, and then the green man comes on. After enough time for you to cross the road, the green man goes off again, and the traffic lights change to green.

▶ Automatic pedestrian crossings make it much safer to cross the road.

This activity will enable you to set up the controls for the green man, using a counter from your electronics kit. You will also need the pulse unit, which sends out a steady stream of pulses (the sequence 0, 1, 0, 1 and so on). This is very useful for driving the counter. A diagram of this circuit is shown in Figure 9.8 on page 90.

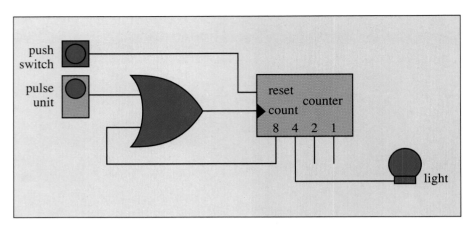

▶ Figure 9.8: Pedestrian crossing control circuit.

▶ An electronics kit connected as a pedestrial crossing controller.

1 Connect the pulse unit on your electronics kit to one input of the OR gate, and the 8 output of the counter to the other OR gate input. Connect the output of the OR gate to the count input. If necessary use the photograph to help.

2 Connect the 4 output of the counter to the output light (which represents the green man).

3 Make sure that there is a push switch attached to the reset input of the counter. This is the button to press to start the crossing control.

4 Make sure that the pulse unit is set for a slow stream of pulses.

5 Press the start switch and watch carefully what happens.

6 Copy and complete the truth table below to describe how the pedestrian crossing controller is working.

Input Start button	Counter 8 4 2 1	Output Light
1	0 0 0 0	Off
0	0 0 0 1	Off
0	0 0 1 0	...
...	...	...
0	1 0 0 0	Off

7 Explain how the OR gate makes the counter stop when it gets to 1 0 0 0 (8).

8 Using the AND gate, modify the circuit so that the light flashes on and off. Add a buzzer which sounds when the light flashes.

9 If you press the start button while the counter is still running, it resets itself and then starts again. Work out a way of modifying the circuit (undoing the flashing light modification, as you will need the AND gate) so that it can only start a cycle after the previous one is finished.

Draw a diagram of the complete modified circuit, and explain how your modification works.

ACTIVITY 9C

Chemical Reaction

▶ A chemical reaction vessel, showing the electronic control panel. This enables the reaction to run continuously without constant supervision.

The chemical industry is one of the major users of electronic control systems. Chemical reactions for making products such as plastics, fertilisers, petrol and glass are monitored and controlled automatically. They can be left running safely for long periods without someone watching over them all the time. If something goes wrong, they are shut down automatically, and an alarm goes off to alert a supervisor.

In this activity you will set up a circuit to control a reaction, and then extend it to monitor how long the reaction takes.

Reaction Controller

The circuit to control the reaction has a main switch and a temperature sensor as inputs. The temperature sensor sends out a 0 if the temperature is below a certain level, and a 1 if it is above it. The output is a relay switch which turns on the heater inside the reactor vessel. The heater is on if the main switch is on and the chemicals are below a certain temperature. It is switched off when the required temperature is reached.

1   Connect the circuit as shown in Figure 9.9. Use the photograph to help you. If you can, connect another circuit (such as a battery and a light bulb) through the relay to simulate the operation of the heater.

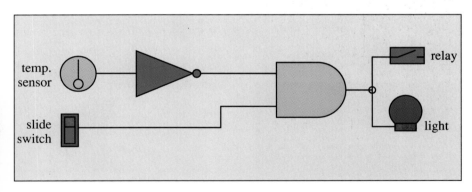

▶ Figure 9.9: Circuit to control a chemical reaction.

▶ An electronics kit set up as a reaction controller.

2   Test the circuit by switching the main switch on and listening for the relay switch to click. Then hold your finger against the temperature sensor. When the sensor warms up, you should hear another click as the relay switches off. With the main switch off, the relay should not move, whether the temperature is high or low.

3   It is rather difficult to know whether the relay is on or off. Add an indicator light which comes on when it is on. Repeat the tests on your circuit.

4 Copy and complete the truth table to describe how the circuit is working.

Inputs		Output
Main switch	Temp. sensor	Relay/Light
0	0	...
0	1	...
1	0	...
1	1	...

Reaction Monitor

One important check on a reaction of this nature is the length of time it takes for the reaction to reach the temperature at which the heat is cut off. This can be done by the circuit in Figure 9.10. The output is the binary number from the counter converted to a base sixteen (hexadecimal) number.

5 Without undoing the reaction control circuit, set up the circuit in Figure 9.10. Use the photograph to help you.

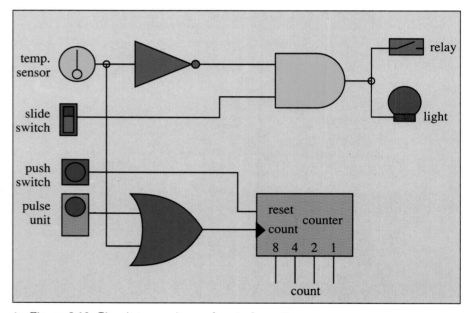

▶ Figure 9.10: Circuit to monitor a chemical reaction.

▶ An electronics kit set up to monitor a chemical reaction.

6 Adjust the pulse unit to produce pulses at about one second intervals.

7 When the temperature sensor is below its changeover point, press the counter reset button, and watch what happens.

8 After a few seconds, hold your finger against the temperature sensor until it passes its changeover point. Again watch what happens.

9 Repeat steps 7 and 8, waiting different periods of time before heating the temperature sensor.

10 Check that the heater circuit switches off at the same time as the timer stops.

11 Copy and complete the truth table below to describe how the reaction timer works.

Inputs		Counter	Output
Reset	Temp. Sensor	8 4 2 1	Display
1	0	0 0 0 0	0
0	0	0 0 0 1	1
0	0	0 0 1 0	2
...	...	...	...

ACTIVITY 9D

Timer

▶ Electronic timers can be used on their own as stopwatches, or as part of control systems.

▶ An electronics kit set up as a press-button timer.

Timers can be used for many purposes, and often form essential parts of control systems. In this activity, you will construct three versions of a timer, using a counter circuit. These can be used in Activity 9E, as well as in the exercises and for projects.

The first type of timer uses a press-button switch. It times while the switch is held down, and stops when it is released. There is a separate reset button.

1 Connect up the circuit shown in Figure 9.11. Use the photograph to help you.

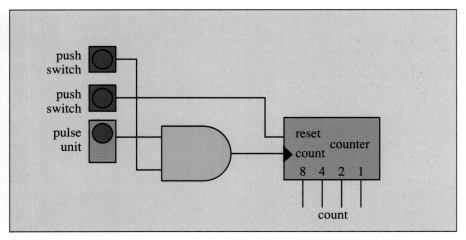

▶ Figure 9.11: Push-button timer circuit.

2 Adjust the pulse unit so that it produces pulses at the rate of about one per second.

3 Press and release the reset button. Then hold down the timing button and, after a short while, release it. Watch what happens.

4　Repeat the previous step a few times, until you are sure that your timer is working properly.

5　Now modify your timer to use a slide switch instead of a pressure switch for the timing. When the switch is on it times; when the switch is off it stops. Again test it until you are sure that it is working properly.

6　Change the modified version of your timer to become an interval timer. This waits a fixed interval (eight time units is most suitable), and then stops. You will need to use the OR gate. Connect the buzzer to sound when the timer reaches the end of the interval.

7　Draw the circuit for your interval timer, and write down the truth table to explain how it works.

ACTIVITY 9E

Disco Light Controller

▶ Disco lights like these are controlled electronically. The lights go through sequences which are set up beforehand.

▶ Electronics kit set up as a disco light controller.

If you have a **memory module** for your electronics kit, one of the things you can do with it is to set it up as a disco light controller. The memory contains a set of **cells** (16 is sufficient), each of which stores a pattern of four binary digits. Each memory cell is identified by a number known as the **addresses** of the cell.

The memory address is connected to the counter so, as you count up, you look at each memory cell in turn. The pattern of bits in the cell you are looking at shows up as coloured lights, these will represent your disco lights. There is a set of switches which enables you to write a particular pattern to the memory cell you are looking at.

1　Connect the memory module to the counter module, and plug in the batteries. Use the photograph to help you.

2　Press the counter reset button and note that the address changes to 0000. At this stage the contents of cell 0000 can be any pattern.

3　Use the slide switches to select a suitable pattern, and press the memory write button to place it in cell 0000.

4   Press the count button to move to the next cell (cell 0001). Choose a suitable pattern and write it to this cell.

5   Repeat step 4 until you have placed a pattern in each memory cell.

6   Now connect one of the timer circuits from Activity 9D to control the counter.

7   Start the timer going and watch the pattern of lights. Adjust the speed of the pulse unit until the pattern is most effective.

8   Disconnect the timer and change the pattern in the memory cells. Re-connect the timer to test them.

9   If you have a suitable relay module which can connect to the memory cells, you can connect up circuits for a larger set of lights.

IT FEATURE

Microchips for Control Systems

Electronic control systems similar to the ones you have designed in the activities in this chapter are used very widely, and more and more applications are being found for them all the time. They are made from **microchips**, similar to those used in computers and digital communications systems. A microchip (also called an **integrated circuit**, or just a **chip**) is a small slice of silicon, on which are formed a large number of electric circuits. These circuits include transistors, which can act as logic gates. A typical microchip contains tens or hundreds of thousands of transistors.

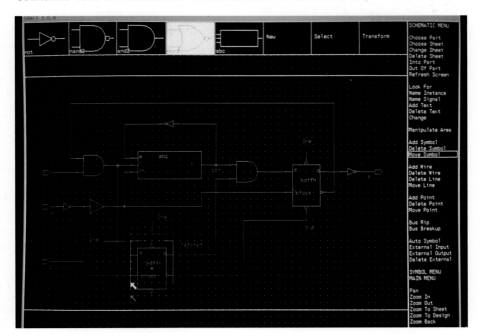

▶ Microchips for specific applications are designed from schematic diagrams like the ones in this chapter.

▶ The operation of a microchip is simulated before it is constructed. The photograph shows the signals going into and out of the chip.

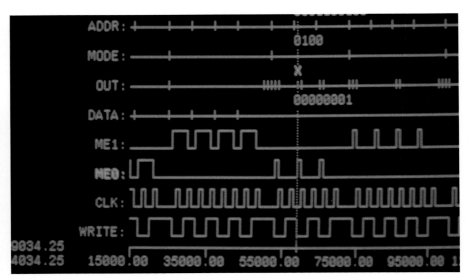

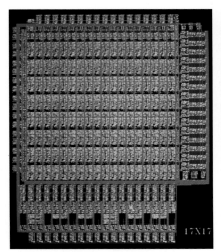

▶ The layout of the silicon chip is often produced automatically by computer. It is shown (greatly enlarged) on the computer screen.

▶ The complete silicon chip in its package. It does the work of a large number of small, general-purpose chips.

▶ Microchips in action — a portable compact disc player.

Microchips for control systems are designed and produced by electronics engineers using computer-aided design (CAD) systems. Once the function of the control system has been decided, a series of logic circuits, like the diagrams in this chapter (but a little more complicated) are entered into the CAD system. When they are all complete, and have been checked, the design is then **simulated** by sending signals into the inputs, and observing what happens at the outputs. These signals are shown graphically as waveforms on the computer screen, and are also output as truth tables. The engineers check these waveforms and truth tables very carefully to make quite sure that the chip will do what they want it to.

Finally the CAD system transforms the logic diagrams into an arrangement of transistors on silicon, connected together to function just like the original logic circuits. This layout is then used in the production of the chips. The chips are tested against the simulation results, and ones which show even the slightest error are rejected.

In this way, microchips designed for a particular purpose can be produced very cheaply, even if the quantities which are made are quite small. They are known as **application-specific integrated circuits** (**Asics**). Some of the more popular uses for chips of this nature are controlling cameras, lifts, automatic doors, machines and robots in factories, washing machines, hi-fi sets and compact disc players. Asics are also used in the control of motor cars, trains, aircraft, satellites and missiles, and in the navigation systems of ships.

The importance of microchips in these applications is that they are small, cheap, and reliable, and they use very little electricity. They are replacing older control systems which took up more space, used more power, and broke down far more often. They are making many things possible which were not practical (or too expensive) in the past. One of the best examples of this is compact discs, which depend on small, powerful microchips for their operation.

Microchips are also changing the way we work, and the way we live. Automatically controlled machines and robots are replacing people in some factory jobs, and making things such as 24-hour banking using cash terminals possible.

TOPIC

Safety of Electronic Control Systems

The Airbus A330 is the first passenger aircraft to use electronic controls throughout. Controls operated by the pilot are inputs to these electronic systems, which then decide how to adjust the rudder, engine speeds and control surfaces on the wings. All control units are duplicated — up to nine times for the most critical ones — and independent microchips compare their outputs, in order to eliminate any which are faulty.

▶ The Airbus A330 is the most advanced passenger aircraft in operation. Its entire control system is electronic, with all important parts duplicated for safety.

This is an example of a system where people's safety depends directly on the correct operation of an electronic control system. It is not the only one, however. Hospitals make increasing use of electronics in patient care, heart pacemakers are electronic systems, and nuclear power stations have electronic control and safety systems, to name a few more examples.

The microchips used in systems such as these are designed and tested with extreme care. Many of them have self-checking circuits which allow them to be tested while they are in use. As in the Airbus, critical systems are often duplicated. Nevertheless, it is difficult to be sure that these systems are completely safe. The safety record of electronic control systems is, in general, good. As systems become more complex, and even more dependent on electronics and less on people, it is increasingly difficult to ensure that these safety standards are maintained.

EXERCISE 9

Questions

1 The automatic gates on the London Underground have three stages in their operation, which are typical of many control systems. They are:

sense — the magnetic strip on your ticket
decide — whether your ticket is valid
act — to open the gate or display a message.

Describe these three stages — sense, decide and act — for each of the following control systems:

(a) central heating system controlled by a thermostat

(b) automatic pilot on a ship

(c) control system on a refrigerator

(d) automatic focusing system on a camera.

2 (a) Make a list of electronic systems on which people's safety depends, in addition to those mentioned in the text.

(b) Choose one of these systems, and make a list of the advantages and disadvantages of using microchips, from a safety point of view.

3 (a) Copy and complete the truth table below for the logic diagram in Figure 9.12.

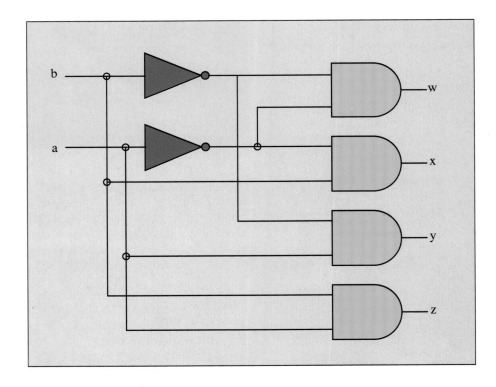

▶ Figure 9.12: Logic diagram for Question 3.

Inputs		Outputs			
a	b	w	x	y	z
0	0	...	...	...	...
0	1	...	...	...	...
1	0	...	...	...	...
1	1	...	...	...	...

(b) Explain briefly what this circuit does.

(c) Suggest at least two uses for this circuit as part of a control system.

Things to Do

1 Draw a diagram for a circuit which has, as output, a light, which flashes when a main switch is on, and is otherwise off. Connect up this circuit using your electronics kit, and check that it works.

2 Many automatic doors open when a light beam is broken by someone approaching. Use the light sensor in your electronics kit as one of the inputs of a control system for an automatic door, and a slide switch as the other input. The door opens when the switch is on and the light beam is broken. Connect a relay switch as the output which controls the door, and also connect a buzzer which sounds when the door is open.

Draw a diagram of the control circuit, and write out a truth table to show how it works. Check the operation of your circuit against the truth table.

3 Most central heating systems are controlled by a thermostat which switches the heating on when the temperature falls below a certain level, and off when the temperature rises above this level.

(a) Set up a logic circuit with a main switch and a temperature sensor as inputs, and a relay switch and indicator light as outputs. The heating is switched on if the main switch is on and the temperature is below a certain level.

(b) Use the counter as a timer for the central heating system. The heating is timed on for a certain interval, and then off for the same length of time. When the heating is timed on, the temperature sensor switches it on as in part (a). You do not need a main switch as the timer is run by the pulse unit set at a suitable slow speed.

Draw circuit diagrams for parts (a) and (b), and a truth table for part (a). Check that the circuits for both parts work as you would expect.

4 Many factories which produce large numbers of identical items use conveyor belts to move the things they produce from one place to another. It is easy to set up an automatic counter for the items by shining a light beam across the belt, and having a sensor to detect when the beam is broken.

▶ Modern central heating systems have electronic controls.

▶ A factory production line in operation — the items produced are identical, making it possible to control production and carry out tests automatically.

Set up a counter for a factory production line, using a light sensor as the input to a counter. Turn the hexadecimal counter into a decimal counter by making it reset whenever it reaches ten (use the fact that ten is eight AND two to help you design it).

Draw the circuit for your counter, and check that it operates correctly.

5 If your electronics kit has a **music module** which connects to the memory output, you can make it play simple tunes by following the method for the disco light controller, Activity 9E. Different patterns in the memory produce different notes. Connect the music module to the memory module and try them out first to hear what they sound like. Then draw up a table of the notes you want in the memory to make up your tune. If you want a long note, you can store it in two or more consecutive cells.

Load the table of notes into the memory, and then connect a suitable timer to the memory address lines. When you start the timer off, you should hear your tune being played.

6 A traffic light follows a fixed sequence, which in Britain is usually green, amber, red and then red and amber together. If the memory module of your electronics kit has lights of these colours, you can set it up as a traffic light controller, following the steps of Activity 9E.

If you set the pulse unit to one second intervals, you will have 16 seconds for the whole cycle. Decide how many seconds you want for each of the four phases, and load the required patterns into the memory. For example if you want red for five seconds, you must load the pattern for red into five consecutive memory cells.

Connect up a timer to cycle through the memory cells, and check that the sequence is what you want.

You may be able to extend your circuit to switch a white light on and off and sound a buzzer while the red light is on. This simulates a pedestrian crossing light.

▶ Music synthesisers are all-electronic. They make sounds using circuits of the type you are designing in this chapter.

▶ The traffic lights in many cities are controlled electronically. Some are connected to a central computer which regulates the flow of traffic throughout the entire city.

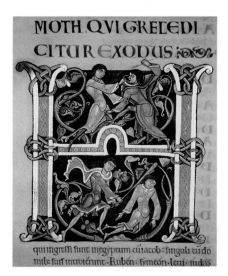

An illuminated manuscript — written and illustrated by hand, taking months to produce a single copy.

For several centuries, the publishing of books, magazines, leaflets and other printed material has been a slow process. It has stayed much the same ever since the invention of the printing press. The overall steps are shown in Figure 10.1. The process can take a week for a magazine, and up to a year for a book.

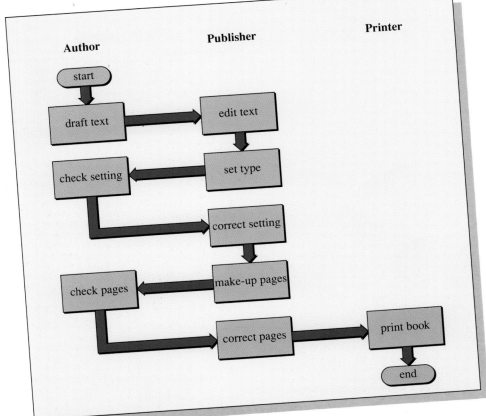

Figure 10.1: The steps involved in publishing a book, using the traditional process.

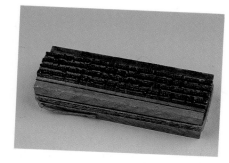

An early example of a printed book and a block of moveable lead type. Each of the letters was cast individually in lead and tied together in blocks for printing.

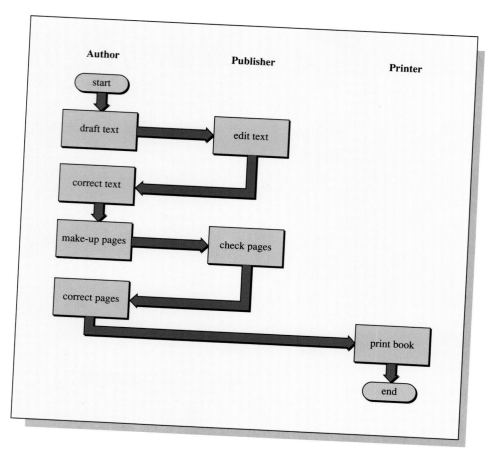

Author   Publisher   Printer

▶ Figure 10.2: The steps in the use of a desktop publishing system to produce a book or magazine.

Now that **desktop publishing** (abbreviated to **DTP**) is available on microcomputers, there is no longer the need for the cumbersome traditional process. See Figure 10.2. A DTP system enables you to:

▶ Plan the design of your publication: the page size and layout (number of columns, width of margins, etc.).

▶ Select the **typefaces** you want for the various headings, main text, figure captions, etc. Each typeface comes in a range of sizes, and often in italic and bold variations. Figure 10.3 gives some examples of popular typefaces.

▶ Take in text from a word processor (or electronic mail system, spreadsheet, database or a range other software), arrange it in the columns, and select the typefaces you want for various parts of it.

▶ Make corrections to the text, and enter small amounts of additional text. Some DTP systems include a full word processor, so you can enter the text straight into the final form of the document.

▶ Take in illustrations from drawing programs or scanned photographs, and re-size or crop them to fit the available spaces. Some DTP systems include drawing facilities.

▶ Draw lines and boxes on the page to separate columns of text or diagrams.

▶ Save your publication on disk and print it. DTP systems use laser printers which give sharp images of text and illustrations.

Some popular typefaces:

New Century Schoolbook 15 point	New Century Schoolbook 10 point
Times Roman 15 point	Times Roman 10 point
Courier 15 point	Courier 10 point
Helvetica 15 point	Helvetica 10 point
Script 15 point	*Script 10 point*

The points measure the height of the type: 72 point type is 1 inch high.

▶ Figure 10.3: Some popular typefaces in different sizes.

It is quite possible for one person to take a publication through all of its stages — entering text and diagrams, designing the pages, setting the type, placing the illustrations, checking and printing. However, it is more common for small teams to do the work, but jobs within the team need not be fixed. The flexibility of the DTP system leads to great flexibility of working arrangements.

Desktop publishing is one of the fastest-growing IT applications. Combined with electronic mail, it makes publication anywhere in the world in a short space of time a practical possibility. Most newspapers in the UK are now produced on DTP systems, and a growing number of magazines are changing over. An increasing number of books, particularly technical books, are produced on DTP systems. The majority of documents produced within businesses — reports, manuals, slides for presentations, etc. — are created with the aid of DTP.

The benefits of DTP are reduced publication time and lower costs, as fewer people are required for the various stages. The disadvantage has been the loss of jobs in the printing industry, and the virtual disappearance of certain traditional crafts.

▶ Some examples of magazines produced by means of desktop publishing systems.

ACTIVITY 10A | *Business Letterhead*

▶ A selection of business letterheads. Each is designed to reflect the style and image of the company.

Businesses use pre-printed stationery for their letters. These **letterheads** give the company name and address, telephone and fax number, and sometimes additional information such as the names of the directors, the VAT registration number, etc. The design of the letterhead also attempts to reflect the image and style of the company. For example, an undertaker would have a very different style of letterhead from an advertising agency.

The aim of this activity is to produce a letterhead for an imaginary company. You need first to decide the nature of the company, and a suitable name and address, and then design the letterhead to reflect the style of the company. The entire design can be done on your desktop publishing program. There is no need to use a separate word processor.

1 Working individually or in pairs, choose a company to design a letterhead for. Look at existing company letterheads if you can collect some, but be original. Try to create the image of a company you would like to work for.

2 Sketch some ideas on paper. Include lines and boxes if appropriate, and use the bottom as well as the top of the page if you wish. Mark out the area to be occupied by the text of the letter.

3 Start your desktop publishing program running, and open up a new publication. Set the page size to A4 (standard letter size) if this is not done automatically.

4 First draw any lines or boxes you require. You may find that you are able to create a grid on your page to help you lay things out.

5 Then change to typing mode, and type the text you need (the company name, address, etc.). Position the text roughly to start — do not worry if it is not quite in the right place, or in the right typeface.

6 Now highlight the text, a line at a time if necessary, and give it the typeface and type size you want. Try a few different typefaces, to see what they look like.

7 Move the text into position, aligning it with the lines and boxes. These may have to be moved or enlarged to fit the text.

8 Add any finishing touches such as simple shapes like ticks or stars, and shade in any areas which require it.

9 Save your letterhead on disk, giving it a file name, and print it.

10 Away from the computer, check the print carefully. It is surprising how many mistakes can occur in the few lines of an address! Mark up any corrections you wish to make.

11 Return to the computer, start up the DTP program if necessary, and call up your publication. Make the corrections, check them on screen, and print the corrected version.

Earthworm

Local Environment Services
23 Puddle Lane
Ahsfield RD4 5TT
Telephone 234 8765
Telex 3459876
Fax 4567654

▶ A business letterhead on the screen as it is being designed using a DTP program.

ACTIVITY 10B *Programme for School Event*

▶ Some examples of programmes for school events produced on desktop publishing systems.

A school event such as a play or sports day benefits greatly from a properly produced programme. Desktop publishing makes this possible within the school, at a fraction of the cost of getting it done by a printer. The aim of this activity is to produce a programme, either for an actual school event (or one at a local youth club or community centre), or for one you have made up.

1 Working in groups of two or three, choose a suitable event.

2 If it is an actual event, you will have to work closely with the organisers to get all the information you need. If not, and you have chosen a play, use a text of it to get the cast list, and then cast your friends as suitable characters. Otherwise make up an appropriate set of information.

3 Make notes of all the facts you need: the title of the event, the date(s) and time(s), admission prices, booking arrangements, telephone number(s) for further information, etc. Also compose some background notes about the event: the history of the play, or the number of years that the sports day has been held for, etc.

4 Plan the overall layout of the programme. It is likely to have about four pages. Decide what is to go on each.

5 Use the word processor on your school computer to enter all the information. Start with the headings for each page, then fill in the details. (Do not worry if the information for one page takes more or less than a page of your word processor. The page layout is set out when you transfer the text to the DTP program.)

6 Save the text on disk, print it, and check it carefully. Make any corrections on the word processor before continuing. Remember that the later in the process an error is spotted, the more difficult and time-consuming it is to correct it.

7 Using the drawing program, enter any drawings that are needed. For example, if your school has a crest and motto, try to draw this on the drawing program. (If the crest is complicated, it may be better to nominate an expert on the drawing program to enter it and then give copies to the other groups.)

8 Print the drawings and check them carefully. Errors spotted and corrected at this stage save a lot of time later. Correct the drawings back at the computer.

9 Now start up the desktop publishing program. Choose a suitable page size — A5 (an A4 page folded in half) is a good size for a programme.

10 Decide on the overall page layout — width of margin, number and width of columns of text, any lines across the top or bottom, page numbers, etc. — and enter these in the page grid.

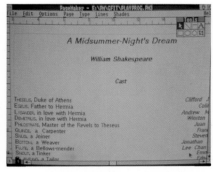

▶ A programme for a school play being set on a desktop publishing system.

11 Bring in the text from the word processor. Look at the instructions for the DTP program to find the method for this. Place the start of this text at the beginning of the programme, and let it flow down the columns and pages.

12 Starting at the beginning of the text, highlight one or more lines at a time, and choose the typeface and type size for them. Centre the text where appropriate, and set tabs to space out any columns. Continue this process until you get the information you want on the correct pages.

13 Break the text to create spaces for illustrations. Bring these in, crop and size them if necessary, and place them in position.

14 Draw in any additional lines or boxes which are required, and shade in any areas for effect.

15 Save the programme on disk and print a draft of it. Check it carefully away from the computer. Mark up any errors in the text or illustrations, and in the way the material is set out. If the programme is for an actual event, make a few copies of it for the organisers, and let them check it.

16 Errors in the drawings must be corrected using the drawing program, and the revised drawings brought back into the DTP program. Simple errors in the text can be corrected in the desktop publishing program, as can errors in the alignment and setting.

17 When you are quite satisfied that all the errors have been corrected, save the final copy of the programme on disk and print it.

ACTIVITY 10C — *School Magazine*

Activity 2B showed you the steps of producing an article for a school magazine using a word processor. Activity 7A covered the process of exchanging articles with another school by electronic mail. Activity 5A described the process of illustrating a news article using a drawing program. This activity brings the things created by these separate activities together, into a complete school magazine, ready for printing.

It is an ambitious activity, best undertaken by groups of at least five pupils. Although this process is done overnight in the offices of every daily newspaper, a longer period of time needs to be allocated for the school version, and a sensible deadline set for production. However, once the deadline has been set, there are no excuses for missing it!

1 To start with, divide into groups of a suitable size, and study some examples of existing magazines: some school magazines and a range of others. Note how the pages are set out, how headings are done, how illustrations are used with the text, and the length of the articles. See if you can detect a style of writing which is common to the articles.

▶ A school magazine produced on a desktop publishing system.

2 Then decide what type of magazine you are going to produce. Possibilities are a class newsletter for the term, a local or national news magazine, or something more specialised, covering a topic such as holiday reports, short stories, poetry, hobbies, etc. Discuss the possibilities thoroughly amongst the group. Once you have decided, you must not change your minds. Also set a target length for your magazine, between eight and 16 pages is reasonable.

3 It is an idea to share out responsibilities for the different aspects of the work. Some members of the group can be reporters/writers, others illustrators, one person can do the overall page design, and one or two can do the actual setting. It is a good idea for everyone to be editors, taking it in turn to check and correct others' work.

4 The first task is to write or collect the text of the articles. Decide on a suitable writing style, and follow the steps of Activity 2B to produce the text of the articles on the word processor, and Activity 7A to exchange articles by electronic mail. Edit any articles you have collected or received by electronic mail, to bring them into line with the style you have chosen.

5 As soon as the drafts of the articles are available, the illustrators can follow Activity 5A to draw suitable illustrations. If you have a scanner, photographs can be taken and scanned at this stage.

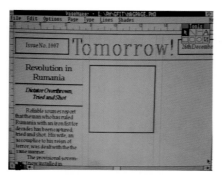

▶ A school magazine being produced on a desktop publishing system.

6 In the meantime, the page designer can start on the page layouts. It is suggested that an A4 page size is chosen, with two or three columns of text.

7 The name of the magazine needs special attention. It is either printed in a carefully chosen typeface, with suitable artwork around it, or drawn by the illustrator using the drawing program. The result, placed at the top of the front page, is known as the **masthead.**

8 When all the separate parts of the magazine — text, illustrations, page design, and masthead — are complete, let each member of the group take it in turn to check them very carefully.

9 When all the errors have been corrected, start the process of setting them in the pages. Follow the steps of Activity 10B for this. The illustrations can generally be enlarged or reduced to adjust the length of each article. If this does not work, articles must be edited, to lengthen or shorten them, to get a good fit in the available space.

10 Save the first draft of the complete magazine, and print it. Again take turns to check the draft carefully.

11 When all the corrections have been made, save and print the final version of the magazine.

IT FEATURE

Laser Printer

Desktop publishing needs an output device which can print text and illustrations of a high quality, quickly, quietly, and reasonably cheaply. The **laser printer** meets these requirements very well. Using a powdered ink, it prints a fine matrix of dots (300 dots per inch both vertically and horizontally). You have to look very carefully to see the pattern of dots; from normal reading distance the output looks crisp and clear. Laser printers are quiet, and fairly quick. The first were somewhat expensive, but prices are falling all the time, without any reduction in quality. At present they do not print in colour.

Laser printers (as well as **Winchester disks** to store the large programs and files which are used for desktop publishing) are the two peripheral devices which have made DTP a practical possibility. Desktop publishing has been one of the fastest growth areas in IT during the 1980s, and its growth looks like continuing during the current decade.

▶ A laser printer, used for output from desktop publishing.

EXERCISE 10

Questions

1 Give some reasons for the popularity of desktop publishing.

2 Why are laser printers so suitable for desktop publishing?

3 Why are Winchester disks essential for desktop publishing?

4 What types of publication are commonly produced using DTP?

Things to Find Out

1 Find out if any local companies or newpapers use desktop publishing in their work. If so, find out why it was introduced and what benfits it has brought.

2 Find out what publications produced within your school could benefit from being produced on a DTP system (but which are not at present done on one). Choose one of these, and write a short description of how it could be produced using DTP, and what the benefits might be. Also mention any possible problems which might arise.

3 The change from traditional methods to desktop publishing by the major UK daily newspapers was sudden, and somewhat dramatic. There were strikes, pickets, overnight moves to new printing plants, and large numbers of redundancies.

   (a) Find out the main sequence of events.

   (b) Find out which groups of people lost their jobs, and what changes took place in remaining jobs.

   (c) Find out whether any newspapers went out of business during the transition, or any new ones have started up since.

   (d) If you can find an old (pre-1985) copy of one of the papers, compare it with a recent one. What differences are there in the quality of the layout and printing?

   (e) Discuss the events which took place, and list any lessons which you think should be learned from them.

Things to Do

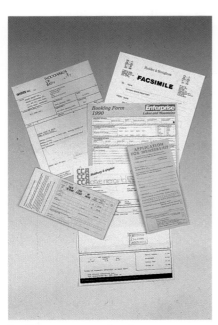

▶ Some common business documents. Producing these is quite possible with a DTP system.

1 Designing and producing business documents, like those shown in the photograph, is often done on a desktop publishing system. The entire task can be carried out using the DTP program. There is no need for a separate word processing or drawing program.

   Choose a business document to design: a form, containing printed information and lines and boxes for things to be written in. The simplest is an invoice (which is filled in when something is purchased from a company). Others include a stock control sheet, a memo or telephone message form, or a booking form to fill in, for example when booking a holiday. Use the ones on the left as examples, and try to obtain some actual business forms to see their designs in more detail.

   Choose a suitable page size (A4 is recommended for most purposes). First draw in the lines and boxes, and then type the text. Move the text into place, and choose a suitable typeface and type size. Add the company logo, and adjust the lines and boxes to fit the text if necessary.

Print a first draft, and check it carefully before entering the corrections and producing the final copy.

2 Use the steps of Activity 10A, 10B or 10C to produce one or more of the following publications:

(a) poster for forthcoming event

(b) menu for restaurant

(c) business card

(d) greetings, birthday, wedding or Christmas card

(e) party invitation

(f) short story with illustrations

(g) information booklet about your school, or a local youth club or community centre

(h) advertising leaflet for an (imaginary) product

(i) personal school timetable.

CHAPTER 11 *Combined Topics*

IT is there to help people get things done. People don't want to use word processors, spreadsheets, databases, graphics programs, electronic mail, viewdata, desktop publishing systems, etc.; they want to write letters, draw plans, send messages, analyse figures, produce books, arrange holidays, and so on. IT helps to do these tasks, but the task is more important than the technology used to do it. Sometimes the facilities provided by IT do not match what people want to do. This is a major reason for the slow uptake of IT in a number of industries.

In practice, it often takes more than one IT facility to get a task done. Alternatively, a combination of IT and manual work does the trick. You have already used a word processor to prepare text for a desktop publishing program. This type of combination is quite common. Some computers run all their programs in such a way that information can be transferred from one to another whenever required. Others run combined suites of software, generally a combined word processor, spreadsheet and database program, which can interchange information.

The activities in this chapter are designed to show you how several IT facilities can be used together. The tasks are somewhat longer than those in previous chapters. Some of them are suitable for project work, either in computing or in another subject. The steps are given in outline only. Planning the details is an essential part of the work.

▶ A typical modern office, with several items of IT equipment in use, amongst all the paperwork!

ACTIVITY 11A *Share Portfolio*

When a company is set up (or when it expands) it needs money for its buildings and equipment, to get it started until it begins to earn money for itself. One way of raising this money is selling **shares** in the company. People who buy the shares own part of the company, and are entitled to a share (a **dividend**) of the profits it makes.

These shares are bought and sold on **stock markets** in large cities such as London, New York, Paris, Tokyo, Hong Kong and Sydney. If a company is doing well (or people think it will do well in the future), the price of its shares increases. If not, its shares decrease in price. Other factors can influence share prices: strikes, wars, changes of government policy, inflation, even the weather. No one knows for sure what will happen to share prices over a period of time.

People who buy shares generally invest in a few companies which they think will do well. They buy a **portfolio** of shares in these companies. They then receive dividends every six months or every year. If later they sell their shares, they make a profit (or a loss). The purpose of this activity is to set up a portfolio of your own, and see how its value changes over a few months.

You will need viewdata to get the share prices, a spreadsheet to record them and a graphics program to display graphs from the spreadsheet. If possible, you should be able to transfer information from these programs to your desktop publishing program.

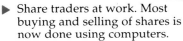
▶ Share traders at work. Most buying and selling of shares is now done using computers.

1 This project can either be done in small groups, or individually.

2 Allocate yourself a sum of money to invest (£10 000 is a suitable figure), and investigate the companies whose shares are on offer, in order to make your choice. The aim is to increase the value of your share portfolio over a period of time. Do not concern yourself with dividends.

3 Spend some time making your choice. Some established companies have prospects of steady growth, while other (generally newer) companies have possibilities of higher growth, but increased risks of losses. Look in the business pages of a newspaper for additional information. Choose between five and ten companies.

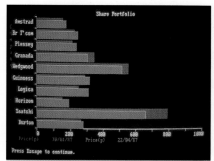

▶ Share prices displayed on a viewdata screen.

4 When you have selected the companies to invest in, call up the share prices on your viewdata program, and 'buy' shares in each, to a total value of the amount of money you have allocated yourself. Write down the purchase prices and quantities of your chosen shares. Open up a word processor document, list the companies in which you have invested, and give brief reasons for your choices of company.

5 Set up a spreadsheet to record your purchases. You must include the date, names of the companies, number of shares in each and purchase price, and get the spreadsheet to calculate the value of the shares in each company, as well as the total value. Choose a suitable layout in rows and columns for this information. Spend some time planning the layout of this spreadsheet, in order to set out all the information as clearly as possible.

6 Once a week, (or once a day if you have the time) call up the share prices on your viewdata program, and write down the selling price of the shares in your chosen companies. Transfer this information to your spreadsheet, calculating the new share values and total portfolio value. Make a note (in your word processor document) of the date and any factors which have influenced share prices during this time.

7 From time to time transfer the total values of your portfolio and the corresponding dates to a program which draws graphs from the figures. Display a line or bar graph of them.

▶ A graph of the change in share portfolio value.

8 If at any stage you decide to 'sell' the shares in a particular company, calculate how much you receive for them, and then 'spend' this money on shares in another company. Work out a way of adjusting your spreadsheet to include this information.

9 At the end of the allocated period of time, print your spreadsheet, and a graph of the changes in the value of your portfolio. Work out the percentage gain or loss on your original investment. Use your notes to produce a report (in a word processor document) on the changes in the prices of your shares, and give reasons (where possible) for these.

10 As an optional extra, bring your report, spreadsheet and graph(s) into your desktop publishing program, and present them as a single publication, set out as a business report.

ACTIVITY 11B | *Experiment Report*

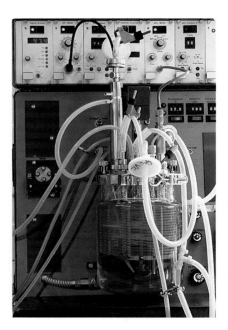

▶ An experiment in an industrial research laboratory. The results are being monitored electronically, and will be fed straight into a computer for analysis.

Most of the experiments conducted at universities and industrial research laboratories are monitored electronically. Measurements are taken automatically at regular intervals and transferred directly to a computer program for analysis. The results are presented as tables of figures and as graphs. Most of the computer programs used for these purposes are written specially for the task.

With the equipment and software available at school, it is possible to carry out experiments in a very similar way. If your school does not have electronic equipment for monitoring experiments, it is possible to take the measurements by hand, enter them into a spreadsheet or statistical program, and use it to do the required calculations and produce the graphs. The report can then be done on a word processor, and all the information brought into a desktop publishing program for final presentation.

▶ A school experiment being monitored by an electronic data recording device. This data can then be transferred to a computer for calculations and output.

1 Working in small groups, choose a suitable experiment. It can be a physics, chemistry, biology or environmental studies experiment. If possible, choose one for which you have a device which can record the results automatically. If this is not possible, choose one where readings are taken at regular intervals, giving a lot of figures over the duration of the experiment.

2 Make sure that you understand the aim of the experiment, and how the equipment works.

   NB: **Be sure to take all the necessary safety precautions, and to wear any protective clothing — gloves, safety glasses, etc. — which is required.**

3 Set up the apparatus and start the experiment running. If you are recording the results automatically, set up the data logger and check that it is operating.

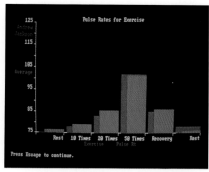

▶ A graph of a set of experimental results, produced on a computer.

4 Take the measurements at regular intervals (or check the data logger if you are using one).

5 At the end of the experiment, transfer your results to a spreadsheet or statistical program, either directly from your data logger, or by typing in the figures.

6 Set up the calculations you need to analyse the results. You may need to calculate averages, or put the numbers into formulae to obtain the information you want. Print the results, and check your calculations carefully.

7 Transfer the appropriate figures to a program which produces graphs of the results. Display and print these, and again check them carefully.

8 On your word processor, draft a report on the experiment. Some suggested headings are:

> Title and date
> Aim of experiment
> Description of equipment
> Operation of the experiment
> Tables of measurements
> Results calculated from the measurements
> Graphs
> Conclusions.

9 Print and check the draft of your report. Make any corrections before continuing.

10 Now bring the tables of results, report and graphs into your desktop publishing program, and set them in a suitable (simple) style. Print a final version of your experiment report.

ACTIVITY 11C *Mailmerge*

▶ When a large number of personalised letters have been produced on a computer, there still remains the problem of putting them all into their envelopes!

In business it is often necessary to send identical letters to a number of people. For example, a company might want to inform its customers of a new product, or an employer might want to send a letter to all employees. These letters look much better if they are properly addressed to each person, rather than photocopied and the name and address typed on later.

Many word processors have a facility for doing this task, taking one basic letter, and a sequence of names, addresses and other particular information, and producing a personalised copy of the letter to each addressee. If necessary, the envelope can be addressed at the same time. The facility is known as **mailmerge**, as it merges a set of names and addresses with the text of a letter. The names and addresses can come from a database, or they can be typed as a separate word processor document.

If your word processor has a mailmerge facility, you can produce a set of personalised letters. There are many uses for these within a school, the most common being to parents, informing them of a forthcoming event at the school.

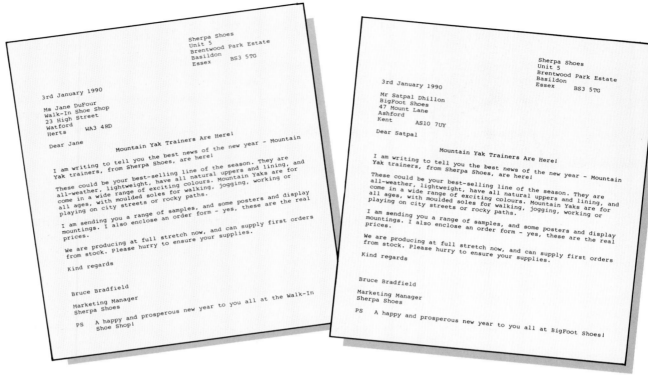

Sherpa Shoes
Unit 5
Brentwood Park Estate
Basildon
Essex   BS3 5TG

3rd January 1990

Ms Jane DuFour
Walk-In Shoe Shop
23 High Street
Watford
Herts   WA3 4RD

Dear Jane

Mountain Yak Trainers Are Here!

I am writing to tell you the best news of the new year – Mountain
Yak trainers, from Sherpa Shoes, are here!

These could be your best-selling line of the season. They are
all-weather, lightweight, have all natural uppers and lining, and
come in a wide range of exciting colours. Mountain Yaks are for
all ages, with moulded soles for walking, jogging, working or
playing on city streets or rocky paths.

I am sending you a range of samples, and some posters and display
mountings. I also enclose an order form – yes, these are the real
prices.

We are producing at full stretch now, and can supply first orders
from stock. Please hurry to ensure your supplies.

Kind regards

Bruce Bradfield

Marketing Manager
Sherpa Shoes

PS   A happy and prosperous new year to you all at the Walk-In
Shoe Shop!

Sherpa Shoes
Unit 5
Brentwood Park Estate
Basildon
Essex   BS3 5TG

3rd January 1990

Mr Satpal Dhillon
BigFoot Shoes
47 Mount Lane
Ashford
Kent   AS10 7UY

Dear Satpal

Mountain Yak Trainers Are Here!

I am writing to tell you the best news of the new year – Mountain
Yak trainers, from Sherpa Shoes, are here!

These could be your best-selling line of the season. They are
all-weather, lightweight, have all natural uppers and lining, and
come in a wide range of exciting colours. Mountain Yaks are for
all ages, with moulded soles for walking, jogging, working or
playing on city streets or rocky paths.

I am sending you a range of samples, and some posters and display
mountings. I also enclose an order form – yes, these are the real
prices.

We are producing at full stretch now, and can supply first orders
from stock. Please hurry to ensure your supplies.

Kind regards

Bruce Bradfield

Marketing Manager
Sherpa Shoes

PS   A happy and prosperous new year to you all at BigFoot Shoes!

▶ Two copies of a letter, produced on a word processor, and each addressed to a different person.

1 Work in groups of two or three, and decide on a topic for your letter, and a group of people to whom you will send it. It can be a letter from the school, or a business letter.

2 Enter a draft of the text of the letter on your word processor. Include the special characters and labels needed at each point where text is to be inserted from the set of names and addresses. See the instructions for your word processor for the method as it varies from one to another.

3 Print your draft and check it carefully. Any mistakes will appear on every copy of the letter! Make all corrections before continuing.

4 Enter a suitable set of (about 10) names and addresses, and any other individual information. Either use your word processor, or a database program. Again consult your manuals for the method and required layout.

5 Print the list of names and addresses and check them carefully. Correct them before continuing.

6 When both the text of the letter and the list of names and addresses have been checked and corrected, run the mailmerge facility. Feed the printer with paper, and watch as the personalised copies of the letter are printed.

7 If anything goes wrong (such as a mismatch between the list of names and addresses and the insertion points in the letter), stop the mailmerge run and make the necessary corrections.

8 When you have finished, write a brief set of instructions so that someone else can carry out the mailmerge operation without having to look up the proceedure in the manuals.

IT FEATURE

Programs in Windows

▶ Most microcomputers can run a number of programs at the same time. Each program occupies a window on the screen. Information can often be transferred from one program to another by cutting and pasting it within the windows.

Not long ago, most microcomputers were restricted to running one program at a time. This is no longer the case, and the most popular way of running several programs is to break the screen into a number of **windows**, one for each program that is running. Windows can be opened and closed as programs start and stop, and be made bigger or smaller, or moved around the screen, while the programs are running. Control is generally via a **mouse**, which moves a pointer around the screen, from one window to another as required.

Most windows environments allow information to be copied from one program to another, via the windows. The commonest method is to highlight an area of information displayed in one window, and copy it into a storage area known as the **clipboard**. The information is then pasted into the window for another program.

Windows make it possible to use computer programs in a much more flexible way than was previously possible. For example, it is possible to run two copies of a word processing program, working on different documents, in two separate windows. The documents can be compared, and text can be transferred between them as required. Similarly, portions of a spreadsheeet can be copied directly into a word processor document to form tables of figures. An electronic mailbox can be opened in one window, and incoming messages cut into word processor documents, and outgoing messages cut from other documents as required. Windows help to overcome the problem mentioned at the start of this chapter — fitting the technology to the requirements of the task, and not the other way round.

EXERCISE 11

Questions

1 Give one reason for the slow uptake of IT in some industries.

2 What is the commonest way of controlling a windows environment?

3 What facilities do windows environments provide?

4 What are the advantages of windows environments?

Things to Find Out

1 If your school computers can run a windows environment, find out what types of programs can be run together in the windows. Make a list of various types of tasks which it might be possible to do using these programs, and the combination of programs required for each task.

Project Topics

The activities in this chapter give the main steps of some tasks which require more than one item of software. Below are some suggestions for further tasks of this nature, which are suitable for projects. These can be computing projects, or projects in the subject which they cover. They are suitable for small groups, or for individual work.

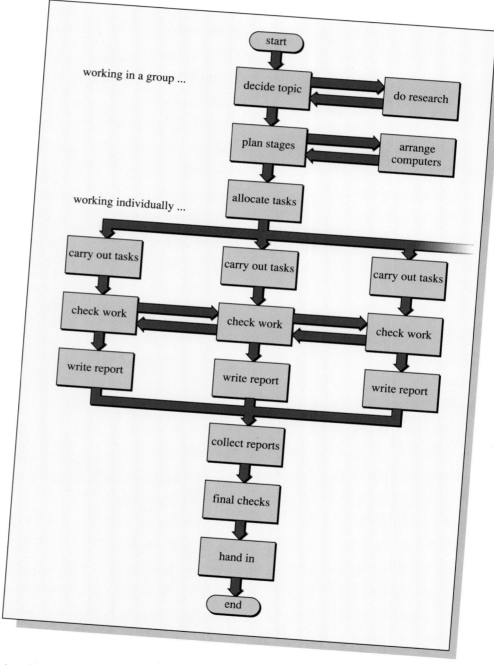

▶ Figure 11.1: A diagram showing the stages of a typical project.

Remember that IT is there to help you get the task done, so you must match the IT facilities to the needs of the task, and not design the project around the capabilites of your computers and software. There is no harm in doing some parts of the project without the aid of a computer, if this is the best method.

For whichever project you choose, you must follow these overall steps:

1   Do some research into the nature and background of the project, to make sure that it is suitable, and to find out where to get any additional information you may need. If the project does not seem suitable after these investigations, choose another one.

2   Plan the overall stages of the project. If it is to be a group project, plan how to divide the work, and set up some deadlines for completing the stages. Make sure that one person cannot hold up all the others if one stage is delayed. It might be helpful to draw a diagram of the stages of the project. See Figure 11.1 for an example.

3   Decide what computer facilities you need for the various stages, and make sure that these are available. Also make sure that you have enough space on disk for the information you need to store.

4   Now set about the task, making sure that you follow the stages you have planned. Keep a record of your progress, and check off deadlines as they are reached.

5   Check each stage carefully before proceeding. The further you go without noticing a mistake, the harder it is to correct it.

6   Keep final reports short and to the point. Quality is much more important than quantity. A few simple diagrams can often improve a report a great deal.

7   Make backup copies of all important information, but keep them up-to-date, and do not allow a great collection of old copies of things to build up. It wastes disk space, and there is a danger of using an out-of-date copy of something, instead of the current one.

Suggested Topics

1   A report on a study you have conducted into an important topic. This may include results of opinion surveys, and any experiments you have done or measurements you have made. The report is done on a word processor, with tables of figures from spreadsheets or statistical programs, graphs from these figures and simple diagrams to illustrate main points. If possible, all the information can be brought into a desktop publishing program for presentation as a single publication.

Topics for a study of this nature include:

(a) A transport study in your area, finding out how people travel to work, to go shopping, to school, etc., and recommending ways of improving the transport network.

(b) A study of employment opportunities for school leavers in your area.

(c) A study of local leisure facilities, both existing ones and others which people would like to have.

(d) A study of a national or international problem, such as the fight against the people who produce, distribute and sell illegal drugs.

(e) An environment survey, taking an area such as a wood, marsh, river or park near you, or one you have visited. Describe the area and the plants and animals which live there, and discuss issues like the effects of pollution or of building developments on it.

(f) A report on a contact you have established with a school in another country. Describe the similarities and differences, both in the school and the general way of life for people of your age. Include copies of correspondence, photographs, etc.

Many studies of this nature form the projects required in a number of subjects. See other subject textbooks for more possible topics.

2 Produce or collect a set of pictures using a drawing program or scanner, and then make them up into a short publication using your desktop publishing program. You may choose a little-known local artist or photographer as a subject. Write a short description of each picture, or a poem to go with it. Plan the layout of the publication to give an overall artistic effect.

NB: Be careful not to break the rules of copyright for any photographs or pictures you scan in. Make sure you state clearly where each image comes from.

3 Produce a database of suitable holidays for your family or your classmates. Use viewdata or holiday brochures as your sources of information, and transfer the details you need onto a database. Write a set of instructions for others to use your holiday database.

4 The combination of computer graphics and a video camera opens up all sorts of possibilities for video productions. The best combination is a graphics program which can take in images from a video camera (or video recorder), and combine them with graphics drawn on the screen. You can build up your images on the computer, and then transfer them as a complete sequence to video tape. A soundtrack can then be added. A few possible topics are:

(a) A children's story, using video film of simple puppets, plus effects drawn by hand.

(b) A documentary film, with video pictures combined with simple diagrams produced on the drawing program. The diagrams are to illustrate the main points of the presentation.

(c) A film based on a theatre or dance performance in the school, with special effects drawn in by hand.

(d) A conventional cartoon, based on hand-drawn cutout figures, with the editing, sequencing and special effects done on the computer.

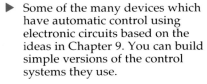

▶ Some of the many devices which have automatic control using electronic circuits based on the ideas in Chapter 9. You can build simple versions of the control systems they use.

5 Many factory robots and similar devices go through a fixed cycle of activities. For example, a robot might: pick up a lid and put it onto a tin; spray-paint a bicycle frame; or fit the wheel onto a car, and tighten the bolts.

The detailed operation of robots like these is beyond the scope of a school electronics kit, but the principle on which they work is often the same as that used in several activities and exercises in Chapter 9. A sequence of control patterns is stored in memory, and a timer runs through successive memory cells. The cycle is either repeated indefinitely, or it stops when it is complete, and is started again when a (reset) button is pressed.

Depending on the output devices you have on your electronics kit, choose a suitable device to construct. For example, if you have a motor-driven Lego kit, and relay switches to control the motors, you might make a simple buggy, crane or robot arm. Work out which memory patterns control the motors in the ways you want. There are normally three patterns, for stop, forwards and backwards.

Then draw up a sequence of controls, using the available memory cells, and repeating the same pattern in successive cells for extended time intervals if necessary. Construct your device, connect up the controls, load the pattern into memory, and connect a suitable timer to activate it. Modify the control patterns, and the speed of the timer, until you are satisfied with the way it works.

Draw a sketch of your design, and the logic circuit which controls it. Write a description of the task your device performs, and the control sequence it uses, and give instructions for someone else to operate it.

6 Set up a viewdata information base to give details on the animals and plants in a particular habitat, such as a pond, wood, field, or even your back garden. Start by studying the area carefully, listing in your notebook all the species you find, where they live, and whether or not you found them in large numbers. Then use a biology reference book to find out some details about them.

Decide on the structure of your viewdata system: the main groupings (possibly insects, plants, birds, land animals, water animals, etc.), and sub-divisions of these groups. Also decide what information to include for each species.

Enter all the information and check it carefully. Produce, on your word processor, a short introduction to the viewdata system, with instructions for its use.

CHAPTER 12 Why IT?

A t the end of the Second World War in 1945, there were about 10 electronic computing devices in use. Today there are tens of millions of computers in operation, and their numbers are increasing all the time. Electronic control systems are becoming increasingly common, and digital telecommunications networks span the globe. This chapter gives some of the reasons for this rapid spread of information technology, and describes the benefits it has brought. It also describes the work involved in the IT industry.

▶ The Colossus codebreaking computer in operation during the Second World War. This enabled the Allies to break the top secret German Enigma codes used for messages sent to submarines and field commanders, and played a decisive role in the eventual Allied victory.

SECTION 12A Benefits of IT

Computers, as we know them today, have been in use for just over 40 years, but information technology has only been in widespread use for the last 15 years, since the development of the microchip in the mid-1970s, and the microcomputer in the early 1980s. During this time, the combination of cheap, powerful computers, advanced telecommunications and electronic control systems has brought about great changes in the way we live and work.

The overall benefit of IT is that it makes people much more effective in their work. One person working on their own, or a small group of people in a team, can now achieve — with the aid of IT — what used to be the work of a large number of people. To get the best out of large teams of people, work had to be broken up into simple, repetitive tasks, making it dull and often unpleasant. Some people had to spend all their time supervising others, without doing

▶ IT has freed large numbers of people from having to work in offices at all. Many can work at home, using a desktop microcomputer and telephone link.

anything productive themselves. Because the technology now takes care of the repetitive details, people can concentrate on the more interesting part of the work. Working arrangements can be far more flexible, both in the type of work done, and in hours worked.

IT enables people to work to much higher standards than before. For example, when a letter was produced on a typewriter, a few mistakes, covered with correcting fluid and over-typed, were usually acceptable. Now, with word processors, letters are corrected on screen and re-printed if there are any mistakes. The higher standard of letters and documents means fewer misunderstandings between people.

IT has had its drawbacks, chiefly in the numbers of people made redundant in factories as robots and electronic control systems were introduced. However, the jobs that were lost were mostly repetitive jobs which required little skill. The overall improvement in economic conditions, due in part to the greater efficiency of IT, has, in most areas, compensated for the initial job losses. The manufacture, distribution and maintenance of IT equipment is a significant industry in its own right, employing large numbers of people. The introduction of IT into offices has led to a re-organisation of jobs, but (contrary to many predictions) few job losses.

The next few sections describe the benefits of the introduction of IT into some specific areas of work. They are some of the most important examples of these developments, but by no means the only ones.

SECTION 12B *IT in the Office*

▶ A typical office scene a century ago. Most paperwork was written by hand, and things took a long time to get done.

▶ The typing pool in a typical office about 25 years ago. Large numbers of women sat for hours behind rows of desks, typing letters and reports.

The place where the changes brought about by IT are most obvious is the office. Gone are the days of the typing pool, where large numbers of women sat behind rows of desks, typing letters and documents all day, for people they never met. Smaller working groups, with flexible working arrangments, and making use of a range of IT equipment and facilities, are now much more efficient. Jobs are more varied and interesting, and part-time working makes it easier for people with families to continue at work. It is also possible for some people to work at home, and communicate with the rest of their work group by telephone, electronic mail and facsimile.

▶ Information technology has made the typing pool obsolete. People in offices have flexible working arrangements, and can get far more work done in less time than in the past.

SECTION 12C

IT in Industry

An area where IT has brought about great improvements in standards is the motor industry. During the 1970s, most vehicle manufacturers were faced with the choice: improve quality and cut costs, or go out of business. Customers were becoming increasingly dissatisfied with the poor quality of cars, and car manufacturers were making huge losses. The solution, adopted to a greater or lesser extent by all car manufacturers, has been to replace their previous production methods by new systems making extensive use of computers and robots. Many built completely new production plants. In the process, thousands of jobs were lost, but quality improved, costs were cut, and the remaining jobs are much more interesting, as well as more secure.

The result is a far greater range of motor vehicles, better designed, better built, and at lower prices than before. Fuel consumption is a fraction of what it used to be, and exhaust pollution is being reduced. The main factor in all these improvements is the widespread use of IT in the design, production and distribution of motor vehicles.

▶ In the past, motor vehicles were assembled by large numbers of workers using simple hand tools. The work was monotonous, quality was poor, and there were frequent strikes.

▶ Today cars are assembled mostly by robots, with small numbers of skilled engineers supervising the production, and carrying out checks. Quality is much higher, costs are lower, and strikes are rare.

The benefits of IT in industry are not restricted to the motor vehicle manufacturing. Steelmaking, glass production, the chemical industry, oil refining, household electrical goods and aerospace are among others which have become more efficient and more profitable, while producing better quality products, thanks to the introduction of IT.

SECTION 12D

Banking and Finance

The banking and insurance industry is another example of the successful application of IT on a large scale. Banks, building societies, credit card companies and insurance companies handle millions of transactions, involving hundreds of millions of pounds, every day. All these transactions are recorded on computer, and many are done by electronic funds transfer, where messages are sent direct from one bank to another with no paperwork. Credit cards, cash terminals and overnight cheque clearance have only come about since the introduction of computers in banking. They would be impossible to operate in any other way.

The result is a great increase in the range services offered by these organisations. Transactions are dealt with quickly, errors are very rare, and decisions (such as whether to give a loan) are made in days, rather than weeks. One problem of being able to get loans more easily is that more people are getting into debt, but the benefits of the improved services outweigh the disadvantages for most people.

▶ Cash on hand around the clock. Cash terminals are only one aspect of the improvement in banking services brought about by IT.

SECTION 12E

Working with IT

The IT industry is one of the fastest growing in the world. It employs large numbers of people as programmers (also known as software engineers), systems designers, electronics engineers, marketing and sales staff, team leaders, project managers and a variety of associated jobs. They design and sell hardware and software, matching the needs of the task to be done with the capabilities of the IT equipment.

Most jobs in IT are highly skilled. They require people with university degrees. The systems which are designed and built are complex, and must be as free of errors as is possible. Many take years to plan, build and test, and can involve teams of tens or even hundreds of hardware and software engineers. There is always great pressure to get the task done, as delays can cost a lot of money, or mean that a competitor gets a similar product on the market first.

▶ An electronics engineer designing a microchip, using a CAD workstation.

▶ Engineers at work in a clean room, manufacturing silicon chips.

▶ An IT project team at a meeting. Communication skills are vital in the IT industry.

Working with IT requires more than just knowledge. The main needs are for clear thinking, an ability to plan the steps of a task, and to work with care all the time. It is also important not to trust results from the computer. These need to be checked very carefully when new hardware or software is being used.

Another important skill is communication, both verbal and written. In any team work, there is much discussion about the details of the work. It is important to make yourself understood, and to understand what others are saying. It is also important to be able to take brief, accurate notes of points made at meetings.

Written records — known as **documentation** — are kept of the design of hardware and software, and **manuals** are produced for the people who use the systems. The documentation is written by the engineers as they design the hardware and software, and is essential for ensuring that the systems are correct and up-to-date. Technical authors are often employed to produce the manuals for the users of the systems. Their job is to describe a complex system in simple language, and make it as straightforward as possible for the users, who may not be computer experts, to operate the system.

A skill for all with ambitions in the IT industry is **management**, that is the ability to get things done by teams of people. There is always pressure of time, and budgets must not be exceeded. The planning, co-ordination, communication and reporting within an IT project team requires skill, experience, patience and hard work.

EXERCISE 12

Questions

1 List **three** benefits of the introduction of IT.

2 (a) What problems faced car manufacturers in the 1970s?

   (b) In what ways did the introduction of IT help to solve these?

3 (a) In which industries has the introduction of IT led to large numbers of job losses?

   (b) How has the introduction of IT lead to increased employment?

4 What changes has IT brought about in offices?

5 What skills are important when working in the IT industry?

6 Look again at the capabilities of IT described in Chapter 1, and at the benefits of its use from this chapter. Taking these into account:

   (a) Choose an area in which IT is used extensively.

   (b) Describe the IT equipment used, and the tasks which it performs.

   (c) Discuss the benefits of the introduction of IT, and any disadvantages. Mention the effects on the people who work within the organisations, and on the people who use their services.

   (d) Give your opinion of future developments in this area, as the power of IT systems increases, and costs fall.

Things to Find Out

1 The **bar code readers** in use at checkouts in most UK supermarkets are visible evidence of a complete change to the use of computers in ordering, distribution, stock control and sales recording that has taken place in most shops in recent years.

   Find out what IT equipment is used in supermarkets and shops, and what tasks it performs. Also find out how the introduction of IT has changed the way the companies operate.

Have there been job losses, and what effects has the change to IT had on prices and profits? What benefits have there been for customers? (Either investigate the situation generally, or choose one shop or supermarket company and use it as a case study.)

▶ The sales assistant is passing the green carton over a bar code reader at a supermarket checkout.

▶ A travel agent making an airline booking at a computer terminal. Airline booking systems were one of the first to be operated directly by the people who used them.

2   Most airline, hotel and package holiday bookings are made on computer systems. There are terminals at travel agents, airports and hotels, all linked to worldwide computer networks. Find out why these computerised booking systems were introduced, and the effects they have had within the travel industry.

3   A modern aircraft, like the Airbus A330, requires only a pilot and co-pilot to operate it. They use a large number of computerised control systems and a range of communications links to assist them in every aspect of the flight. These include planning, weather forecasts and reports, takeoff, navigation, engine control, fuel monitoring and landing.

Find out some details about these on-board IT systems: what tasks they perform, and how much control the pilots have over them. Also find out the reasons for their introduction, and their effects on speed, safety, work within the airline, and costs.

Things to Do

1   Imagine that you were setting up a small shop — selling clothes, household goods, hardware or some other range of goods. At any time there would be a manager and two assistants on duty. Using the information from this chapter, and from Chapter 1:

(a) Decide what items of IT equipment you would need for your shop.

(b) Describe briefly the tasks your IT systems would perform.

(c) List the types of software you would require for these tasks.

(d) Give reasons for your choice of IT equipment and software, and state the benefits you would expect from it.

2   Contact a local company which uses IT in its operations.

   (a) Find out what equipment is used, and the tasks it is used for.

   (b) Find out what changes took place when the new technology was introduced.

   (c) Find out the reasons for the change to IT, and the benefits it has brought.

   (d) Write a report on your findings, pointing out any lessons that were learned in the process of changing to IT.

3   Identify some potential uses of IT within your school. Select three of these, and write a brief report on each, describing:

   (a) the task to be performed by the IT equipment

   (b) what hardware and software is required

   (c) who will operate the system, and what training they will need

   (d) any potential problems which may arise

   (e) the benefits of changing to IT.

Glossary

This glossary lists the meanings of the technical terms in the book. Most concern IT, but a few general terms which might be unfamiliar are also included.

application-specific integrated circuit (Asic)   an integrated circuit designed for a particular purpose, often for a control function.

bar code   a code made up of wide and narrow stripes, most commonly found on packaged goods at supermarkets.

binary   base two.

cash terminal   a device used by banks to dispense cash automatically.

chip   see *integrated circuit.*

clipboard   a temporary storage area, used to transfer information from one program to another in a windows environment.

communications network   a collection of cables, satellite links and exchanges which enable voice and computer messages to be sent from one place to another.

computer   a digital electronic information processing machine which can be programmed.

computer-aided design (CAD)   the use of drawing programs and related computer facilities in the design process.

computer-aided design/computer-aided manufacture (CAD/CAM) direct links between CAD systems and electronically controlled machines.

control system   a device which directs the operation of a vehicle, machine or process.

cursor   an illuminated area on a display screen which indicates where the next typed character is to appear.

daisy wheel printer   a type of printer which uses a rotating wheel to select the characters to be printed.

database   a collection of related information, arranged in a structure which makes it easy to use.

database program   a program which allows a person to search, edit and add to a database.

desktop publishing (DTP)   carrying out all stages in the production of a publication (design, text entry and editing, producing illustrations, page layout and printing) on a single computer system.

digital   information which can be recorded as characters (letters or the digits of numbers).

display screen   a screen, resembling a television screen, used for computer output.

dividend   the share of the profits of a company paid to each shareholder.

document   a letter or other piece of text produced by a word processor.

documentation   a written description of how an item of hardware or software works.

dot matrix printer   a type of printer which produces characters and graphics as patterns of dots.

electronic   describes computers, control systems and communications networks which use integrated circuits for their operation.

electronic document interchange (EDI)   the exchange of commercial documents (purchase orders, invoices, payments, etc.) by electronic mail.

electronic mail   a service for sending and receiving messages between computers via telephone lines.

exchangeable disk   a magnetic disk which can be removed from a disk drive.

facsimile (fax)   the image of a document (text or graphics) which is sent down a telephone line and printed by the receiver.

field   the place for one item of information in a database.

frame   one photograph in a film or video.

gate   a logic processing device which takes one or more input signals and produces an output depending on the values of the inputs.

gateway   a link between one network and another.

graphics   drawings, diagrams, maps and other images produced on a computer screen.

hardware   the physical devices (integrated circuits, printed circuit boards, cables, etc.) which make up a computer or other electronic system.

hexadecimal   base sixteen.

highlight   to emphasise a character, word or area of a display screen by making it brighter.

information   things which we read, see, hear or find out.

information provider   an organisation which provides information for a public viewdata system.

information technology (IT)   the combination of computers, control systems and communications networks, all based on digital electronic devices.

input   information which goes into a computer or control system.

integrated circuit (IC)   a device made from a small piece of silicon, on which are formed a number of processing, storage or other circuits.

integrated services digital network (ISDN)   the range of voice, computer message and other services provided by a digital communications network.

inventory   a list of items of equipment.

invoice   a commercial document showing a list of goods which have been purchased, and how much is to be paid for them.

keyboard   an input device consisting of a number of keys, including letter, number, punctuation and control keys.

laser printer   a printer using powder ink and a laser beam, printing both text and graphics and giving a high quality of printed image.

local network   a network of computers, terminals and other devices in the same room or building.

logic circuit   a circuit made up of gates and storage elements, together performing a logic operation.

long distance network   a network connecting computers over long distances, generally via telephone lines or satellite links.

machine   a device which does useful work.

magnetic disk   an information storage medium, with information stored as small magnetised areas.

magnetic disk drive   a device which writes information to a magnetic disk, and reads it from the disk.

mailbox   the storage area for incoming messages to a user on an electronic mail system.

mailmerge   the facility for combining a standard text with lists of names and addresses to produce personalised copies of letters.

memory   the part of a computer where information is stored while it is in use.

memory address   a number which identifies the place where an item of infomration is stored in memory.

memory cell   the storage space for one item of information in a computer memory.

microchip   see *integrated circuit*

microcomputer   a computer based on a processor made from a single microchip.

microprocessor   a processing device made from a single microchip, used in a computer or control system.

modem   a device which links a computer to a telephone line.

mouse   a hand-held input device which is moved against a surface to move a pointer or highlight on the display screen.

network   a set of computers, terminals and other digital devices connected by communications links.

network cable   the physical link between devices on a network.

number field   the space for a number in a database record.

optical disk   a storage medium for information in terms of small indentations on a glass surface, which are read by a laser beam.

output   information which comes out of a computer or control system.

page   one screenful of information on a viewdata system.

palette   the set of available colours on a colour graphics system.

pixel   one dot in a graphics image on a display screen or printed page.

plotter   an output device which plots drawings, plans, maps, etc.

printer   an output device which produces printed copies.

processing   the operations carried out on information by a computer.

processor   the part of a computer where information is processed.

program   a set of instructions which control the operation of a computer or other programmable device.

purchase order   a commercial document that lists items which are to be purchased.

qwerty keyboard   a keyboard in the conventional typewriter layout, the top left keys start with the letters q, w, e, r, t, y...

record   one set of related information in a database.

relay switch   a switch controlled by a small electric current, which opens or closes a circuit carrying a much larger electric current.

resolution   the degree of detail in a graphics image.

retrieval   locating an item of information in a database.

scanner   a graphics input device which copies pictures into a computer.

server   a computer on a network which controls a magnetic disk, printer or other resource which is shared by all the workstations on the network.

share portfolio   a collection of shares in different companies.

silicon   the material, found in sand, from which integrated circuits are made.

simulation   forecasting the behaviour of an integrated circuit before it is constructed, by analysing its logic circuit.

software   the set of programs which control the operation of a computer or other programmable device.

software engineer   a person who designs, writes and tests computer programs.

spreadsheet   a table of numbers, formulae and other information set out in rows and columns.

spreadsheet cell   the space for one numnber, formula or other item of information in a spreadsheet.

storage   recording information in a form in which it can later be retrieved.

stylus   a graphics input device, similar to a pen, which is moved over a tablet, moving a point on the display screen in the process.

systems designer   a person who designs IT systems.

terminal   an input device giving direct access to a computer.

terminal network   a network connecting a number of terminals to a central computer.

text field   the storage space for an item of text in a database.

thermostat   a temperature sensor which switches a signal on if the temperature is above a certain level, and off if it is below the level.

truth table   a table showing the inputs and corresponding outputs of a logic circuit or gate.

typeface   a set of characters in a particular printing style.

viewdata   a set of information stored in terms of screen pages, which are accessed by users, often over a network.

waveform   the pattern of inputs and outputs produced by an integrated circuit or similar device.

Winchester disk   a fixed, high-capacity magnetic disk.

windows environment   a method of running several programs at the same time on a computer, with each program having a window in the display screen for input and output.

word processor (WP)   a computer program for the entry, editing, storage, retrieval and printing of text.

workstation   a computer connected to a network, making use of the servers for disk storage, printing, etc.

Index